Australia

Travel Guide

2025

The Complete Traveler's Handbook to Discover the Hidden Gems, Historic Villages, Must-See Attractions and Insider Tips for an Unforgettable Experiences

Reed M. Callahan

Copyright Notice

No part of this book may be reproduced, written, electronic, recorded, or photocopied without written permission from the publisher or author.

The exception would be in the case of brief quotations embodied in critical articles or reviews and pages where permission is specifically granted by the publisher or author.

Although every precaution has been taken to verify the accuracy of the information contained herein, the author and publisher assume no responsibility for any errors or omissions. No liability is assumed for damages that may result from the use of the information contained within.

All Rights Reserved ©2025

TABLE OF CONTENT

INTRODUCTION	9
OVERVIEW OF AUSTRALIA	10
WHY VISIT AUSTRALIA?	11
BEST TIME TO VISIT	13
KEY TRAVEL TIPS	15
CHAPTER 1: PLANNING YOUR TRIP	19
VISA AND ENTRY REQUIREMENTS	19
HEALTH AND SAFETY PRECAUTIONS	21
CURRENCY AND PAYMENTS	23
TRAVEL INSURANCE	25
PACKING TIPS	27
CHAPTER 2: GETTING AROUND AUSTRALIA	31
FLIGHTS AND AIRPORTS	31
PUBLIC TRANSPORTATION (BUSES, TRAINS, TRAMS)	34
RENTING A CAR AND ROAD TRIPS	37
DOMESTIC FLIGHTS AND FERRIES	40
CYCLING AND WALKING	43
CHAPTER 3: ACCOMMODATION OPTIONS	47
HOTELS AND RESORTS	47
LUXURY HOTEL	47
MID-RANGE HOTEL	55
HOSTELS AND BUDGET STAYS	63
HOSTELS	63

Budget Stays	71
Airbnb and Vacation Rentals	79
Luxury and Eco-Friendly Lodging	86
Campgrounds and Glamping	95

CHAPTER 4: TOP DESTINATIONS — 103

Sydney: Iconic Landmarks and Hidden Gems	103
Melbourne: Culture, Art, and Food	105
Brisbane and the Gold Coast: Beaches and Outdoor Adventures	107
Cairns and the Great Barrier Reef	109
Perth: Sunset Views and Coastal Life	112
Adelaide: Wine Regions and Festivals	114
Hobart and Tasmania: Wilderness and Heritage	116
Darwin: Outback Adventures and Indigenous Culture	118

CHAPTER 5: MUST-SEE ATTRACTIONS — 121

Sydney Opera House and Harbour Bridge	121
Uluru (Ayers Rock)	123
The Great Barrier Reef	125
Great Ocean Road	127
Kakadu National Park	129
The Twelve Apostles	131
Fraser Island	133
The Whitsundays	135
National Parks and Wildlife Sanctuaries	137

CHAPTER 6: OUTDOOR ACTIVITIES — 139

Hiking and Bushwalking	139
Surfing and Beach Activities	141
Scuba Diving and Snorkeling	143

SNORKELING WITH WHALE SHARKS	145
CAMPING AND WILDERNESS ADVENTURES	147
CYCLING AND ROAD TRIPS	149
INDIGENOUS EXPERIENCES AND CULTURAL TOURS	151

CHAPTER 7: AUSTRALIAN CULTURE — 153

INDIGENOUS CULTURE AND HISTORY	153
AUSTRALIAN CUISINE AND FOOD CULTURE	155
FESTIVALS AND EVENTS	157
SPORTS AND RECREATION	159
THE ARTS AND MUSIC SCENE	161

CHAPTER 8: SHOPPING IN AUSTRALIA — 165

SOUVENIRS AND INDIGENOUS CRAFTS	165
MARKETS AND FLEA MARKETS	167
LUXURY SHOPPING	171
BEST SHOPPING DISTRICTS	173

CHAPTER 9: FOOD AND DINING — 177

AUSTRALIAN CUISINE: WHAT TO TRY	177
INDIGENOUS FOOD AND BUSH TUCKER	190
TOP RESTAURANTS AND DINING EXPERIENCES	192
CAFES AND STREET FOOD	195
REGIONAL SPECIALTIES	197
NIGHTLIFE AND BARS	200

CHAPTER 10: PRACTICAL INFORMATION — 205

LANGUAGE AND COMMUNICATION	205
CURRENCY AND TIPPING	207
EMERGENCY NUMBERS AND HEALTHCARE	209
INTERNET AND SIM CARDS	212
TIME ZONES AND WEATHER	215
ELECTRICAL PLUGS AND VOLTAGE	218

CHAPTER 11: SUSTAINABLE TRAVEL IN AUSTRALIA — 221

ECO-FRIENDLY TRAVEL PRACTICES	221
RESPONSIBLE TOURISM GUIDELINES	223
WILDLIFE PROTECTION	226
SUSTAINABLE ACCOMMODATIONS AND ECO-TOURS	228

CHAPTER 12: DAY TRIPS AND SHORT ESCAPES — 233

BLUE MOUNTAINS FROM SYDNEY	233
GREAT BARRIER REEF FROM CAIRNS	235
YARRA VALLEY WINE TOUR FROM MELBOURNE	238
PHILLIP ISLAND PENGUIN PARADE	240
TASMANIA DAY TRIPS	242

CHAPTER 13: 7-DAY CLASSIC AUSTRALIA ITINERARY — 247

DAY 1: ARRIVAL IN SYDNEY	247
DAY 2: SYDNEY EXPLORATION	250
DAY 3: FLY TO CAIRNS & GREAT BARRIER REEF	253
DAY 4: DAINTREE RAINFOREST & CAPE TRIBULATION	256
DAY 5: FLY TO MELBOURNE	259
DAY 6: MELBOURNE DAY TRIPS	262
DAY 7: MELBOURNE TO SYDNEY AND DEPARTURE	266

CHAPTER 14: RESOURCES AND USEFUL LINKS — 269

Tourism Websites — 269
Emergency Services — 273
Language Resources — 275
Transportation Booking Sites — 278
Travel Blogs and Forums — 282

CHAPTER 15: CONCLUSION — 285

Final Tips for Traveling in Australia — 285
Embrace the Aussie Spirit — 287
Staying Safe and Enjoying the Journey — 288

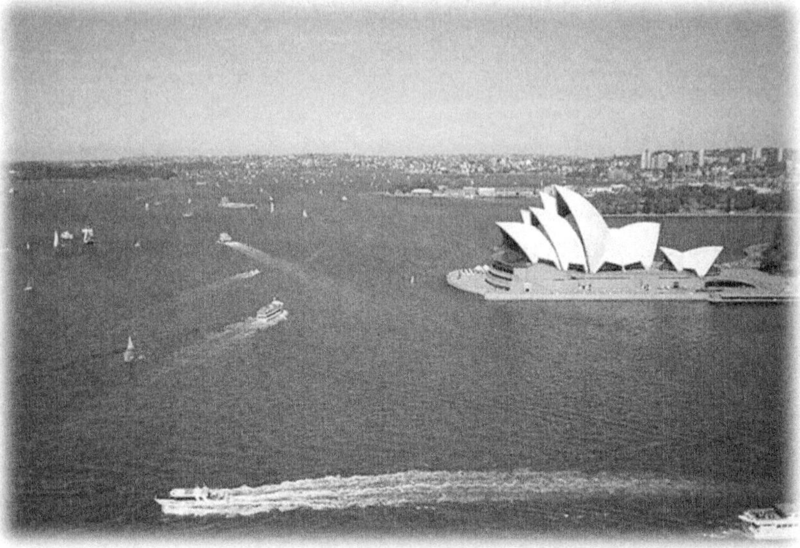

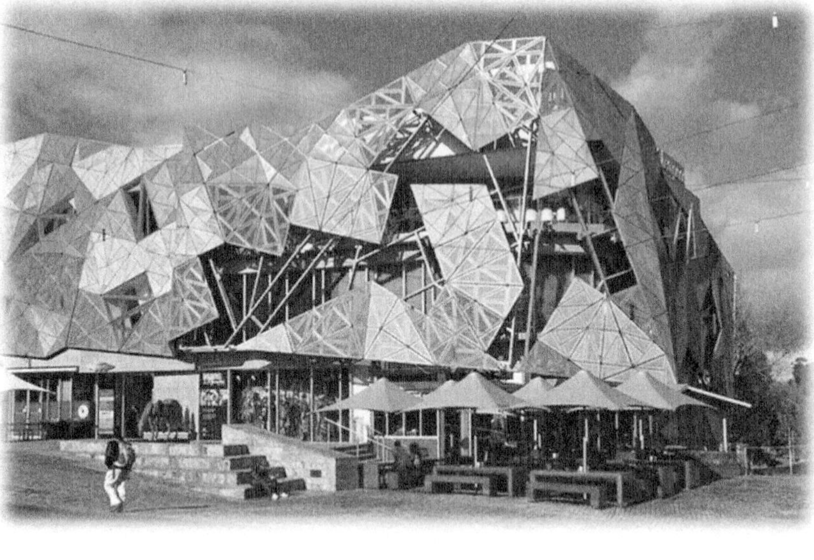

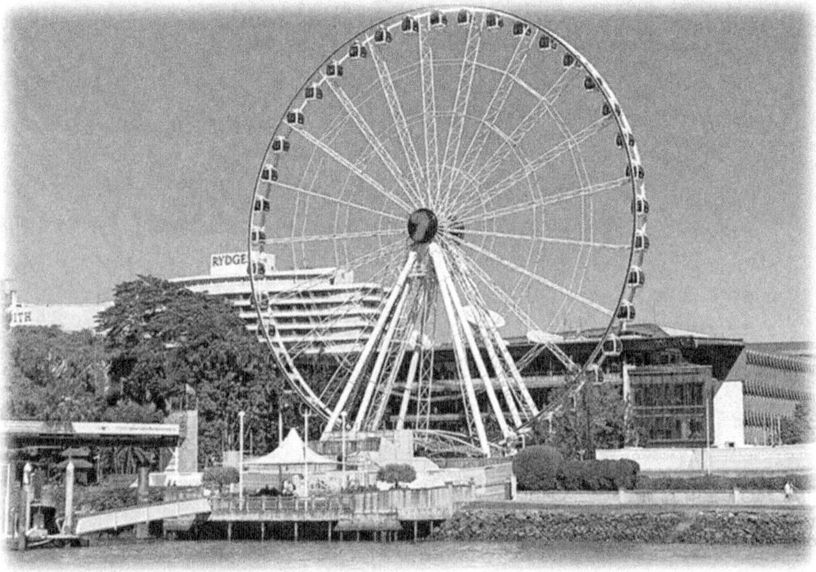

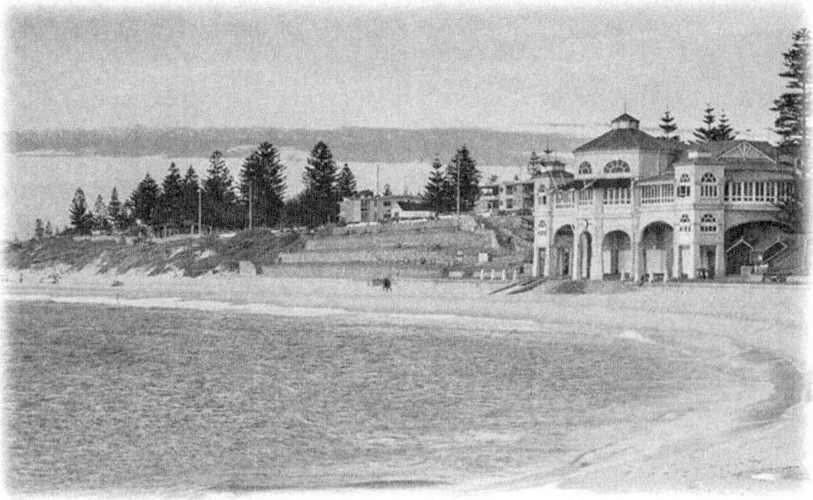

INTRODUCTION

Are you overwhelmed by the endless travel options in Australia? Confused about visa requirements and entry rules? Wondering how to pack efficiently for a land of deserts, beaches, and lush rainforests? Worried about how to get around in such a vast country? Unsure about where to find the best accommodations for your budget? Curious about hidden gems beyond the well-known attractions? Struggling to plan a trip that balances adventure, relaxation, and culture? Concerned about sustainable travel and responsible tourism? Looking for insider tips that go beyond typical guidebooks?

If you answered yes to any of these questions, you've come to the right place. *Australia Travel Guide 2025: The Complete Traveler's Handbook* is designed to make your journey stress-free, enjoyable, and unforgettable. Packed with practical advice, insider recommendations, and curated itineraries, this guidebook ensures you'll have all the tools to explore Australia like a pro.

From the iconic Sydney Opera House to the breathtaking Great Barrier Reef, the vibrant food scene in Melbourne, and the unspoiled wilderness of Tasmania, we'll take you through Australia's top attractions, unique experiences, and local treasures. Whether you're hiking through national parks, diving with whale sharks, savoring Indigenous cuisine, or discovering boutique markets, this guide is your trusted companion.

Dive into these pages and let us help you create a trip that goes beyond expectations. It's time to embrace the Aussie spirit, explore responsibly, and craft memories that last a lifetime.

Overview of Australia

Australia, the world's sixth-largest country, is both a continent and a nation, known for its stunning natural beauty, diverse ecosystems, and rich cultural heritage. Spanning 7.69 million square kilometers, it is home to iconic landmarks, vibrant cities, and vast wilderness areas that captivate travelers from around the globe.

Geography

Australia boasts a varied landscape, from the arid outback and red sands of Uluru to lush rainforests in Queensland and the pristine beaches of the Great Barrier Reef. The country is divided into six states and two territories, each offering unique experiences. Coastal regions are home to bustling cities like Sydney and Melbourne, while the interior, or "the bush," offers a rugged charm that's perfect for adventurers.

Climate

Australia's climate varies significantly due to its size. The north experiences tropical weather, with warm temperatures and monsoonal rains, while the south enjoys a temperate climate with four distinct seasons. The outback regions are hot and dry, creating starkly beautiful desert landscapes.

Culture

Australia's culture is a blend of Indigenous traditions and multicultural influences. The Aboriginal and Torres Strait Islander peoples have a history dating back over 65,000 years, and their art, music, and storytelling remain an integral part of the nation's identity. Modern Australia is also shaped by waves of immigration, making it a melting pot of cultures, languages, and cuisines.

Wildlife

Famous for its unique wildlife, Australia is home to species found nowhere else, including kangaroos, koalas, platypuses, and wombats. Its ecosystems range from coral reefs teeming with marine life to eucalyptus forests where diverse birds and marsupials thrive.

Economy and Lifestyle

Australia ranks high in quality of life, education, and healthcare. Known for its laid-back lifestyle, Aussies embrace outdoor activities, sports, and a love of nature. The country is a global leader in wine production, and its culinary scene blends fresh local ingredients with international flavors.

Why Visit?

Australia offers something for every traveler—relax on idyllic beaches, explore cosmopolitan cities, dive into vibrant Indigenous culture, or embark on epic road trips. Whether you're seeking adventure, relaxation, or cultural immersion, Australia's unparalleled beauty and welcoming spirit make it a destination you'll never forget.

Why Visit Australia?

1. Natural Wonders

Australia is home to some of the world's most iconic landscapes, including the Great Barrier Reef, Uluru (Ayers Rock), and the Twelve Apostles along the Great Ocean Road. Its diverse ecosystems span tropical rainforests, arid deserts, pristine beaches, and snow-capped mountains, providing countless opportunities to marvel at nature's splendor.

2. Unique Wildlife

Where else can you encounter kangaroos, koalas, wombats, and platypuses in their natural habitats? Australia's wildlife is unlike anywhere else on Earth, with hundreds of species found only here. National parks and wildlife sanctuaries offer unforgettable encounters with these amazing creatures.

3. Vibrant Cities

From Sydney's stunning harbor and Melbourne's artistic flair to Brisbane's sunny vibe and Perth's coastal charm, Australia's cities blend modern attractions with unique character. Each urban center offers world-class dining, cultural events, and nearby natural escapes.

4. Adventure Opportunities

Australia is an adventurer's paradise. Dive or snorkel in the Great Barrier Reef, surf world-class waves, hike through ancient rainforests, or camp under the stars in the Outback. Whether you're into adrenaline-pumping activities or peaceful exploration, Australia delivers.

5. Indigenous Culture

Discover the world's oldest continuous cultures by engaging with Aboriginal and Torres Strait Islander traditions. Experience Indigenous art, music, and storytelling, and join guided tours to learn about their deep spiritual connection to the land.

6. Culinary Delights

Australia's food scene is a melting pot of flavors. Relish fresh seafood, indulge in world-class wines from regions like Barossa Valley and Margaret River, and taste native bush tucker inspired by Indigenous traditions. From fine dining to vibrant street food, there's something for every palate.

7. Laid-Back Lifestyle

Australia's relaxed and welcoming vibe makes it easy to enjoy your trip at your own pace. The locals, often referred to as "Aussies," are known for their friendly and approachable nature, ensuring you'll feel at home wherever you go.

8. Endless Sunshine and Stunning Beaches

With over 10,000 beaches, Australia is a haven for beach lovers. Whether you're lounging on Bondi Beach, exploring the Whitsundays, or watching sunsets in Broome, the coastal scenery is simply breathtaking.

9. Sustainability and Conservation

Australia is a leader in eco-tourism, with a commitment to preserving its natural treasures. Visitors can participate in sustainable travel experiences, including wildlife conservation tours and eco-friendly accommodations.

Best Time to Visit

1. Seasons in Australia

Summer (December to February): Warm to hot temperatures, ideal for beaches and outdoor activities. Best for exploring coastal regions, the Great Barrier Reef, and vibrant cities like Sydney and Melbourne.

Autumn (March to May): Milder weather, perfect for sightseeing, wine tours, and hiking. Great for visiting the Outback, national parks, and regions like the Barossa Valley.

Winter (June to August): Cool temperatures, particularly in the south. Best time for skiing in the Australian Alps and exploring tropical regions like Cairns and the Great Barrier Reef.

Spring (September to November): Pleasant temperatures and blooming landscapes. Ideal for outdoor adventures, wildlife encounters, and events like the Melbourne Cup.

2. Regional Highlights by Season

Northern Australia (Tropical Climate)

Dry Season (May to October): Perfect for visiting Cairns, Darwin, and the Great Barrier Reef. Enjoy clear skies and pleasant temperatures.

Wet Season (November to April): Heavy rains and high humidity but excellent for waterfalls and lush greenery. Some areas may be inaccessible due to flooding.

Southern Australia (Temperate Climate)

Summer (December to February): Great for exploring beaches, festivals, and outdoor events in cities like Sydney, Melbourne, and Adelaide.

Winter (June to August): Cooler weather, perfect for indoor attractions like museums, wine regions, and cozy retreats in Tasmania.

Central Australia (Desert Climate)

Winter (May to September): Mild days and cool nights make it the best time to explore Uluru, Alice Springs, and the Red Centre.

Summer (October to April): Extremely hot, with temperatures often exceeding 40°C (104°F), which can make outdoor activities challenging.

3. Special Events and Festivals

Summer: Sydney New Year's Eve Fireworks, Australian Open in Melbourne, and Surfing competitions along the coasts.

Autumn: Adelaide Fringe Festival, Melbourne Food & Wine Festival, and whale watching on the east coast.

Winter: Vivid Sydney light festival, Dark Mofo in Tasmania, and snow sports in the Australian Alps.

Spring: Melbourne Cup, Floriade flower festival in Canberra, and wildflower blooms in Western Australia.

General Recommendations

For Beaches and Coastal Adventures: Visit during summer (December to February).

For the Outback and Desert Adventures: Opt for cooler months (May to September).

For Nature and Wildlife: Spring (September to November) is ideal for wildflowers and animal activity.

For Budget Travelers: Travel during the shoulder seasons (March to May or September to November) for fewer crowds and lower prices.

Key Travel Tips

1. Plan for Australia's Size

Australia is enormous, and travel between destinations can take hours or even days. Focus on specific regions or cities if you have limited time, rather than trying to see everything.

Use domestic flights for long distances and consider road trips for exploring smaller regions.

2. Prepare for the Climate

Pack according to the region and season you're visiting. Layers are essential for varying temperatures, especially in the desert or coastal areas.

Don't underestimate the sun. Bring sunscreen, a wide-brimmed hat, and sunglasses to protect yourself from harsh UV rays.

3. Respect Wildlife and Nature

Observe wildlife from a safe distance and avoid feeding animals.

If you're visiting national parks or beaches, follow guidelines to protect fragile ecosystems.

4. Check Visa and Entry Requirements

Most travelers need an Electronic Travel Authority (ETA) or eVisitor visa to enter Australia. Apply online well before your trip.

Ensure your passport is valid for at least six months from your date of entry.

5. Stay Connected

Buy a local SIM card or portable Wi-Fi device for reliable internet access. Major providers include Telstra, Optus, and Vodafone.

In remote areas, mobile coverage can be limited, so download maps and offline guides beforehand.

6. Budget Wisely

Australia can be expensive. Save money by using public transport, cooking some of your own meals, and exploring free attractions like beaches and national parks.

Dining out? Tipping is appreciated but not mandatory, as service charges are often included.

7. Drive Safely

Australians drive on the left side of the road. If you're renting a car, familiarize yourself with local road rules.

Be cautious in remote areas where wildlife may cross the road, especially at dawn and dusk.

8. Embrace the Local Culture

Learn a few Aussie phrases and slang terms—it's a great icebreaker with locals.

Respect Indigenous customs and traditions. When visiting sacred sites like Uluru, follow guidelines to ensure cultural sensitivity.

9. Be Aware of Wildlife Risks

Australia's wildlife is fascinating but can also be dangerous. Learn about potential hazards, such as jellyfish, snakes, and spiders, especially if venturing into the wild.

Always swim between the flags at beaches to avoid strong currents and marine hazards.

10. Stay Hydrated and Protected

Carry a reusable water bottle, especially when hiking or exploring remote areas. Tap water is safe to drink in most regions.

Use insect repellent to avoid bites, particularly in tropical areas where mosquitoes are prevalent.

11. Pack Smart

Bring comfortable walking shoes, a waterproof jacket, and swimwear to suit a range of activities.

An international power adapter (Type I) is necessary for most travelers.

12. Download Essential Apps

Use apps like Google Maps, TripView (for public transport in Sydney), and Wi-Fi Finder to navigate and stay organized.

Chapter 1: Planning Your Trip
Visa and Entry Requirements

1. Determine If You Need a Visa

Most travelers need a visa to enter Australia, regardless of their trip's purpose.

Citizens of New Zealand may enter visa-free but must hold a valid passport and meet specific eligibility criteria.

2. Common Types of Australian Visas

Tourist Visa (Subclass 600): For tourism, visiting family, or attending short-term courses. Valid for up to 12 months.

eVisitor Visa (Subclass 651): For travelers from eligible European countries. Free and allows stays up to 3 months.

Electronic Travel Authority (ETA) (Subclass 601): For travelers from eligible countries, including the USA, Canada, and Japan. Apply via the Australian ETA app.

3. How to Apply

Apply online via the **Australian Government's Department of Home Affairs** website or mobile app for ETAs.

Provide required documents such as a valid passport, travel itinerary, proof of funds, and health insurance (if applicable).

Processing times vary, so apply well in advance of your travel date.

4. Passport Validity

Your passport must be valid for at least six months from your planned date of entry.

5. Health Requirements

Some travelers may need to provide proof of vaccinations, especially if coming from countries with a yellow fever risk.

Australia has strict biosecurity laws. Declare all food, plant, and animal products on arrival to avoid fines.

6. Entry Restrictions

Ensure you meet character requirements (no serious criminal convictions) and health standards.

Be prepared to show proof of return tickets and sufficient funds to support your stay.

7. Customs and Quarantine

Australia has strict customs rules to protect its unique environment. Declare all items, including food, plants, and animal products.

Fines apply for undeclared restricted items.

8. Immigration Clearance

Upon arrival, present your passport, completed incoming passenger card, and visa.

SmartGates are available for eligible passport holders to speed up the clearance process.

9. Travel Insurance

While not mandatory, travel insurance is highly recommended to cover medical emergencies, trip cancellations, and unexpected delays.

Health and Safety Precautions

1. Health Precautions

Vaccinations: Ensure routine vaccinations (MMR, DTP, etc.) are up to date. No special vaccines are required unless you're arriving from a yellow fever zone, in which case proof of vaccination may be requested.

Travel Insurance: Obtain comprehensive travel insurance that covers medical emergencies, hospital stays, and evacuation, especially if visiting remote areas.

Medications: Bring a sufficient supply of prescription medications and carry them in their original packaging with a copy of your prescription.

2. Sun Protection

UV Radiation: Australia has one of the highest UV levels in the world. Wear sunscreen (SPF 30+), sunglasses, and a wide-brimmed hat.

Stay Hydrated: Carry a reusable water bottle to avoid dehydration, especially during outdoor activities. Tap water is safe to drink in most areas.

3. Wildlife and Marine Safety

Bush Safety: Be cautious of snakes and spiders, especially in rural or wooded areas. Wear sturdy boots and watch where you step.

Marine Hazards: Swim only at patrolled beaches and between the flags. Watch for signs warning of jellyfish, sharks, or strong currents. In northern Australia, stinger nets protect against dangerous jellyfish.

Kangaroos and Other Wildlife: Drive carefully in rural areas to avoid collisions with animals, particularly at dawn and dusk.

4. Food and Water Safety

Safe to Eat and Drink: Australian food and tap water meet high safety standards. In remote areas, confirm water safety or carry purification tablets.

Allergies: Inform restaurants of any dietary restrictions or allergies. Australia has strict food labeling laws.

5. Staying Safe Outdoors

Hiking and Camping: Inform someone of your plans, carry a map and plenty of water, and be prepared for sudden weather changes.

Heat Management: During summer, avoid strenuous activities during peak heat hours (10 AM–3 PM).

Bushfires: Familiarize yourself with bushfire safety, particularly in dry seasons. Check local alerts and avoid high-risk areas.

6. Emergency Preparedness

Emergency Numbers: Dial *000* for police, fire, or ambulance services.

First Aid: Carry a basic first aid kit, especially if traveling to remote areas.

Local Contacts: Note the locations of nearby medical facilities and pharmacies.

7. COVID-19 and Other Health Concerns

COVID-19 Guidelines: Follow current government health advisories regarding vaccinations, mask use, and social distancing.

Mosquito-Borne Diseases: In northern Australia, protect against bites to prevent diseases like dengue fever. Use insect repellent and wear long sleeves in affected areas.

8. Personal Safety

Cities and Urban Areas: Australia's cities are very safe, but stay vigilant, particularly at night. Avoid poorly lit areas and secure your belongings.

Remote Areas: Travel with proper supplies, including water, food, and a fully charged phone or satellite communication device.

Currency and Payments

1. Currency Overview

Official Currency: The Australian Dollar (AUD), symbolized as **$** or **A$**.

Denominations:

Coins: 5¢, 10¢, 20¢, 50¢, $1, and $2.

Banknotes: $5, $10, $20, $50, and $100.

2. Currency Exchange

Where to Exchange:

Exchange cash at banks, airport currency exchange counters, or dedicated foreign exchange outlets like Travelex.

Avoid exchanging large amounts at airports due to higher fees and less favorable rates.

Rates: Check the current exchange rate before exchanging currency to ensure you're getting a good deal.

3. Credit and Debit Cards

Widely Accepted: Visa, Mastercard, and American Express cards are commonly accepted at hotels, restaurants, shops, and attractions.

Contactless Payments: Tap-and-go payments using cards or mobile wallets (e.g., Apple Pay, Google Pay) are very popular.

ATM Access: ATMs are widely available across cities and towns for cash withdrawals. Check with your bank for fees on international transactions.

4. Payment Preferences

Cash vs. Card:

Major cities rely heavily on cards, and cash is less commonly used.

In rural or remote areas, it's wise to carry some cash, as card payment options may be limited.

Small Businesses: Some small businesses may have minimum card payment limits or prefer cash.

5. Tipping and Service Charges

Not Mandatory: Tipping is not a common practice in Australia, as workers are paid fair wages. However, rounding up your bill or leaving a small tip for exceptional service is appreciated.

Service Charges: These are usually included in restaurant and hotel bills, so additional tips are unnecessary.

6. Banking Hours

Typical Hours: Banks are generally open Monday to Friday, 9:30 AM to 4:00 PM. Some may have extended hours or operate on Saturdays in major cities.

Online Banking: Use mobile banking apps for convenience during your trip.

7. Tax Refund for Tourists (TRS)

Eligibility: Tourists can claim a refund on the Goods and Services Tax (GST) and Wine Equalisation Tax (WET) on purchases over $300 from a single retailer.

How to Claim: Present your receipts, goods, and passport at the airport's TRS counter before departing.

8. Currency Safety Tips

Avoid carrying large amounts of cash. Use secure methods like travel cards or credit cards.

Keep small denominations handy for public transport, small purchases, or tipping.

Travel Insurance

1. Why You Need Travel Insurance

Healthcare Costs: While Australia has excellent healthcare facilities, treatment can be expensive for non-residents without insurance.

Trip Interruptions: Coverage for cancellations, delays, or interruptions ensures you won't lose money if plans change unexpectedly.

Adventure Activities: If you plan to engage in activities like scuba diving, hiking, or surfing, ensure your insurance covers these adventures.

Lost or Stolen Items: Protection against lost baggage, passports, or personal belongings provides peace of mind.

2. Types of Coverage to Consider

Medical Coverage: Includes hospital stays, doctor visits, emergency medical evacuation, and ambulance services.

Trip Cancellation/Interruption: Reimburses prepaid expenses if you need to cancel or cut your trip short due to unforeseen circumstances.

Baggage and Personal Belongings: Covers loss, theft, or damage to your luggage and valuables.

Adventure Sports Coverage: Specifically for high-risk activities like diving or trekking.

Rental Car Excess Insurance: Reduces costs if you have an accident with a rental vehicle.

3. Choosing the Right Policy

Coverage Amount: Ensure the policy provides sufficient medical and evacuation coverage (at least AUD $1,000,000 is recommended).

Policy Exclusions: Check for exclusions like pre-existing conditions, alcohol-related incidents, or unapproved activities.

Duration and Multi-Trip Options: Choose single-trip coverage for one visit or annual coverage if you travel frequently.

Provider Reputation: Opt for reputable insurance companies with strong reviews and reliable customer service.

4. Cost of Travel Insurance

Prices vary depending on the level of coverage, your age, trip duration, and planned activities. Expect to pay between 4% and 10% of your trip cost for comprehensive coverage.

5. How to Purchase Travel Insurance

Buy online from insurance providers, travel agencies, or banks. Some airlines also offer policies during ticket booking.

Compare plans on platforms like **InsureMyTrip** or **Squaremouth** to find the best deal.

6. Emergency Contact Information

Keep your policy number and the insurance company's contact details accessible at all times.

Many policies include 24/7 assistance for emergencies like medical issues or travel disruptions.

7. Medicare Reciprocal Agreements

Citizens of select countries (e.g., UK, New Zealand) can access limited Medicare benefits in Australia under reciprocal healthcare agreements. However, these do not replace comprehensive travel insurance.

8. Claiming Insurance

Notify your insurer as soon as an incident occurs.

Provide documentation like receipts, medical reports, or police reports to support your claim.

Packing Tips

1. Understand the Climate

Summer (December–February): Hot temperatures in most areas (up to 40°C or 104°F). Pack lightweight, breathable clothing, sunscreen, sunglasses, and a hat.

Winter (June–August): Milder in southern regions (around 10–20°C or 50–68°F), cooler in northern regions. Bring layers, a jacket, and comfortable shoes for walking.

Rainy Season (November–March): Pack a waterproof jacket and sturdy shoes if traveling to tropical regions like Queensland or the Northern Territory.

2. Pack for Outdoor Adventures

Comfortable Footwear: Sturdy shoes for hiking, walking, and exploring. If you plan to visit national parks or go bushwalking, opt for hiking boots.

Swimwear: Whether you're visiting the Great Barrier Reef or relaxing on a beach, don't forget a swimsuit.

Daypack: A lightweight, waterproof daypack is ideal for day trips and outdoor adventures.

Water Bottle: Carry a refillable water bottle to stay hydrated during outdoor activities.

3. Clothing Essentials

Lightweight and Versatile Clothing: Pack clothes that can easily mix and match for a variety of settings, from casual to semi-formal.

UV Protection: The Australian sun is intense. Pack long-sleeve shirts, hats, and sunglasses to protect yourself from UV radiation.

Layers for Cool Evenings: Temperatures can drop quickly, especially in the evening or in the outback, so bring a lightweight jacket or sweater.

4. Toiletries and Health Items

Sunscreen and Lip Balm: With Australia's strong UV rays, high SPF sunscreen and lip balm with SPF are crucial.

Insect Repellent: Essential for protecting against mosquitoes, especially in tropical areas.

Basic First Aid Kit: Include band-aids, antiseptic, pain relievers, motion sickness tablets, and any personal medications.

Prescription Medications: Bring enough medication for the entire trip, along with a copy of the prescription.

5. Tech and Gadgets

Phone and Charger: Make sure your phone is unlocked if you plan to use a local SIM card.

Power Adapter: Australia uses Type I electrical outlets with a voltage of 230V and frequency of 50Hz. Bring a suitable power adapter and voltage converter if needed.

Camera: If you want to capture the stunning landscapes and wildlife, a camera with a zoom lens is recommended.

6. Travel Documents

Passport and Visa: Ensure your passport is valid for at least six months beyond your arrival date. Carry a printed copy of your visa and other important documents.

Travel Insurance: A copy of your travel insurance policy and emergency contact information should be easily accessible.

Travel Guide/Maps: While mobile apps are useful, having a hard copy of a travel guide or map can be handy, especially in remote areas.

7. Money and Payment Essentials

Local Currency: Bring a small amount of Australian Dollars (AUD) for small purchases or places that don't accept cards.

Credit/Debit Cards: Notify your bank of your travel dates to avoid any issues with international card transactions.

Travel Wallet: Use a secure travel wallet or money belt to keep your cash, cards, and passport safe.

8. Packing Light and Smart

Roll, Don't Fold: Rolling clothes saves space and reduces wrinkles.

Compression Bags: If you need extra space, consider packing with compression bags.

Limit Luggage: Keep your luggage under 20-25 kg (44-55 lbs) to make traveling easier, especially if you plan to take domestic flights with baggage restrictions.

9. Don't Forget the Extras

Snacks: Pack some healthy snacks for long flights or road trips across the country.

Travel Locks: Use locks for your luggage to prevent theft while you're traveling.

Wet Wipes and Hand Sanitizer: Handy for cleaning your hands, especially in remote locations where soap and water may not be readily available.

Chapter 2: Getting Around Australia
Flights and Airports

1. International Flights to Australia

- **Major International Airports**:

Sydney (SYD): Australia's busiest and most international gateway.

Melbourne (MEL): A major hub for international flights, especially from Asia.

Brisbane (BNE): Popular for flights from the Pacific Islands and Asia.

Perth (PER): Serves as a key entry point for travelers from Southeast Asia and the Middle East.

Adelaide (ADL) and **Cairns (CNS)**: Smaller international airports with limited international connections but growing routes.

Flight Duration:

From the US: Around 14-16 hours direct flight (depending on the city)

From Europe: 20+ hours (with a stopover in the Middle East or Southeast Asia)

From Asia: 5-9 hours depending on the departure city

2. Booking International Flights

Major Airlines:

Qantas: Australia's flagship carrier, offering direct and connecting flights to major cities worldwide.

Virgin Australia: Provides both international and domestic services.

Emirates and **Singapore Airlines**: Offer excellent connections from Europe, Asia, and the Middle East to Australia.

Flight Search Engines: Use websites like **Skyscanner**, **Google Flights**, or **Kayak** to compare prices and find the best deals.

3. Domestic Flights within Australia

Popular Domestic Airlines:

Qantas: Offers extensive domestic coverage, from major cities to regional towns.

Virgin Australia: Another major carrier with a comprehensive domestic route network.

Jetstar: A low-cost airline for domestic and international flights.

Rex Airlines: A regional carrier for smaller cities and remote locations.

Flight Duration:

Sydney to Melbourne: 1.5 hours

Sydney to Brisbane: 1.5 hours

Melbourne to Adelaide: 1 hour

Cairns to Sydney: 2.5 hours

4. Airport Facilities

Sydney Kingsford Smith Airport (SYD): Offers a wide range of amenities, including lounges, duty-free shopping, restaurants, and transport links to the city.

Melbourne Tullamarine Airport (MEL): Known for its vibrant food scene, art installations, and convenient transport options.

Brisbane Airport (BNE): Offers a variety of shopping, dining options, and a direct link to the city by the Airtrain.

Perth Airport (PER): A growing international airport with excellent facilities, including lounges and modern shopping.

Other Airports: Most airports in major cities have modern facilities like cafes, stores, and transport options (buses, taxis, and car rentals).

5. Airport Transportation

Public Transport:

Airtrain in Brisbane connects the airport to the city center.

Airport Link in Sydney offers a fast train service to Central Station.

SkyBus provides affordable airport transfers in Melbourne, Sydney, and other cities.

Taxis and Ride-Sharing: Uber, Ola, and taxis are available at all major airports, with designated pick-up zones.

Car Rentals: Available at most airports, with major international brands like Hertz, Avis, and Budget.

Shuttle Services: Many hotels provide shuttle services to and from the airport, so check with your accommodation in advance.

6. Tips for a Smooth Flight Experience

Arrive Early: Arrive at least 3 hours before international flights and 1.5-2 hours for domestic flights.

Customs and Immigration: Upon arrival, you'll go through customs and immigration. Have your passport, visa, and any necessary paperwork ready.

Duty-Free Shopping: Duty-free stores are available at most major airports, where you can purchase goods like alcohol, cosmetics, and luxury items at tax-free prices.

7. Regional and Remote Airports

For travel to regional or remote destinations, domestic flights may be required. Airports like **Cairns** (CNS), **Darwin** (DRW), and **Hobart** (HBA) serve as gateways to natural wonders like the Great Barrier Reef, Uluru, and Tasmania's wilderness.

Many smaller towns are served by regional flights, but they may have limited services, so booking in advance is recommended.

8. Luggage and Customs

Luggage Limits: Domestic flights generally have a baggage limit of 20kg for checked luggage and 7kg for carry-on. International flights may allow more.

Customs Declarations: Australia has strict quarantine regulations, especially for food, plants, and animal products. Be sure to declare any items that may be restricted.

Public Transportation (Buses, Trains, Trams)

1. Buses

Coverage: Buses are the backbone of public transport in Australia, covering cities, suburbs, and regional areas.

City Buses: In cities like Sydney, Melbourne, Brisbane, and Adelaide, buses run frequently and connect all major districts and suburbs.

Intercity Buses: Long-distance buses connect larger cities and regions, such as Greyhound and Premier Motor Service, offering affordable travel between cities like Sydney, Melbourne, and Brisbane.

Payment:

Opal Card (Sydney), **Myki Card (Melbourne)**, **Go Card (Brisbane)**, and other city-specific cards make boarding buses easy. You can top up your card online, at vending machines, or through retailers.

Cash: Some buses still accept cash payments, but this is becoming less common, especially in large cities. It's recommended to use a transport card for convenience and better fares.

Tips:

Plan your journey using local transport apps or websites.

Buses can be crowded during peak hours (7-9 AM and 4-6 PM), so plan accordingly.

2. Trains

City Trains: All major Australian cities have extensive train networks.

Sydney Trains: The network spans throughout the city and to surrounding suburbs. Trains are frequent and comfortable, making them a popular option for commuting.

Melbourne's Metro Trains: Melbourne's train network serves the city and its suburbs with frequent services.

Brisbane and Perth Trains: Both cities have well-developed rail networks connecting central areas with surrounding suburbs and towns.

Long-Distance Trains:

Australia also offers scenic, long-distance trains for travel between major cities.

The Ghan: A legendary rail journey between Adelaide and Darwin, offering stunning views of the outback.

Indian Pacific: Connects Sydney and Perth, offering a unique cross-country journey.

Overland: A train route between Melbourne and Adelaide.

Payment:

Just like buses, city train services use smart travel cards (Opal, Myki, Go Card) or mobile payment options.

Long-distance train services can be booked directly through the railway company websites.

Tips:

Trains are a comfortable and quick way to travel long distances. However, they may not always run on time during peak hours or bad weather.

For scenic long-distance trains, it's advisable to book in advance as they tend to sell out, especially during peak travel seasons.

3. Trams (Streetcars)

Cities with Tram Services:

Melbourne: Known for its extensive tram network, Melbourne's trams are iconic and cover almost every part of the city and surrounding suburbs.

Adelaide: The tram network here is smaller but covers key areas like the city center, beachside areas, and other major destinations.

Payment:

Like buses and trains, trams in Melbourne and Adelaide are accessible using the **Myki card** (Melbourne) or **Metroticket** for single rides.

In Melbourne, a **Free Tram Zone** exists within the central city area where trams are free for travel.

Tips:

Trams are slower than trains but are an excellent way to experience the city's sights.

Trams can get busy during rush hours, especially in Melbourne. Try to avoid traveling during peak periods if possible.

4. Fares and Ticketing

City Transport Cards: Each major city uses a smartcard system (e.g., Opal, Myki, Go Card) for buses, trains, and trams. These cards can be topped up online or at retail locations throughout the city. They offer discounted fares compared to single tickets.

Daily Caps: Some cities offer a daily cap on transport, meaning you'll never pay more than a certain amount for travel each day, regardless of how many trips you make.

Ticket Validation: Remember to tap on and tap off at stations and on buses or trams to ensure you're charged the correct fare. If you forget to tap off, you might incur extra charges.

5. Special Transport Options

Ferries: In cities like Sydney, ferries offer a scenic and convenient way to get around the harbor and nearby areas, such as Manly and Taronga Zoo.

Night Transport: Many cities, including Sydney and Melbourne, offer night buses and trains for travelers. These services are typically less frequent but still operate to key areas, particularly on weekends.

6. Apps and Resources

Transport Apps: Many cities have dedicated apps to help you navigate their public transport systems. Apps like **TripView** (Sydney), **PTV** (Melbourne), and **Brisbane Transport** provide real-time updates, timetables, and journey planning.

Google Maps: Google Maps also offers public transport routes and times across Australian cities, including live updates for delays or disruptions.

Renting a Car and Road Trips

1. Renting a Car in Australia

Rental Agencies: International and local car rental companies, such as **Hertz, Avis, Budget, Europcar**, and **Thrifty**, operate throughout Australia. You can book online in advance or at airport locations.

Age Restrictions: Most rental agencies require drivers to be 21 years or older. Drivers under 25 may incur an additional young driver surcharge.

Driver's License: You'll need a valid driver's license from your home country. If it's not in English, you may need an International Driving Permit (IDP).

Insurance: Basic insurance is usually included, but consider upgrading to reduce excess (the amount you'll pay in case of damage). Always check the policy details.

Deposit: A deposit is typically required when renting a car, which will be refunded if the vehicle is returned in good condition.

Fuel: Cars are usually rented with a full tank of fuel, and you're expected to return the vehicle with a full tank. If not, fuel charges may apply.

2. Types of Vehicles to Rent

Economy and Standard Cars: Ideal for city driving and short trips.

SUVs and 4WDs: Suitable for off-road adventures or traveling in the outback. Some national parks require 4WD vehicles for certain tracks.

Campervans and RVs: Perfect for a road trip across the country, offering the flexibility to camp along the way.

Luxury Vehicles: Available for those wanting a more upscale driving experience.

3. Road Rules and Driving Etiquette

Driving Side: In Australia, you drive on the left-hand side of the road.

Speed Limits: Speed limits are strictly enforced, with typical limits being 50 km/h (city areas), 100 km/h (rural areas), and 110 km/h (highways). Always watch for signs, as limits may vary.

Seat Belts: Seat belts are mandatory for all passengers.

Mobile Phones: Using a mobile phone while driving is illegal unless you have a hands-free system.

Blood Alcohol Concentration (BAC): The legal limit is 0.05%. Drink-driving penalties are severe, including fines and loss of license.

Road Signs and Markings: Familiarize yourself with Australian road signs, including roadworks, wildlife warnings, and other alerts.

4. Road Trips in Australia

Australia offers some of the world's most scenic and diverse road trips. Here are a few popular routes:

The Great Ocean Road (Victoria): This iconic drive takes you along the southern coast with breathtaking ocean views, coastal cliffs, and the famous Twelve Apostles rock formations.

Pacific Coast Way (Queensland): This route stretches from Brisbane to Cairns, offering coastal views, tropical rainforests, and beautiful beaches.

Outback Adventure (Northern Territory and South Australia): Drive through the heart of Australia, from Alice Springs to Uluru, or take the famous Ghan railway route.

The Nullarbor Plain (South Australia to Western Australia): A remote stretch of road, perfect for adventurous travelers seeking isolation and wide-open landscapes.

Tasmania's Great Eastern Drive: Explore Tasmania's east coast with stops at beautiful beaches, wineries, and coastal towns.

5. Road Trip Tips

Plan Your Route: Distances in Australia can be vast, so plan your road trip carefully. It's essential to know how far your destinations are and how long the drive will take.

Fuel and Supplies: Always fill up your tank before long stretches, especially when traveling in remote areas. Carry plenty of water, snacks, and a spare tire.

Weather Conditions: The weather can change quickly, particularly in the outback. Be prepared for hot conditions, sudden storms, and even frost in colder months.

Accommodation: Book your accommodation in advance, especially in remote areas, as options can be limited. Consider camping for a more adventurous experience.

Wildlife and Road Hazards: Watch out for wildlife on the roads, especially kangaroos, emus, and other animals, particularly around dawn and dusk.

6. Parking in Cities

Urban Parking: In major cities like Sydney, Melbourne, and Brisbane, parking can be expensive and limited. Use parking apps to find affordable spots or opt for public transportation if you're staying in the city.

Street Parking: Pay attention to parking signs, as fines for illegal parking are common. Many cities offer free parking in certain areas, typically outside peak times.

7. Returning Your Rental Car

Return Location: You can usually return the car to the same location or a different one, depending on the rental company.

Check for Damages: Before returning the car, inspect it for any damage and take photos. This will help avoid disputes over the car's condition.

Final Charges: Rental agencies will charge for fuel if the tank is not full or if there are any damages.

Domestic Flights and Ferries

1. Domestic Flights

Australia has an extensive network of domestic flights, making it easy to travel between major cities, regional centers, and tourist destinations.

Airlines:

Qantas: Australia's flagship airline, known for its reliability, extensive domestic network, and excellent service.

Virgin Australia: Another major carrier with a competitive range of routes, offering flexible pricing and frequent flyers programs.

Jetstar: A low-cost subsidiary of Qantas, ideal for budget-conscious travelers, though services may be more basic.

Rex Airlines: A regional carrier offering flights to smaller destinations across Australia.

Booking Flights:

Price Comparison: Use flight comparison websites like **Skyscanner**, **Google Flights**, or **Kayak** to find the best deals on domestic flights.

Booking in Advance: Booking ahead of time can help secure lower fares, particularly during peak travel periods (e.g., Christmas, Easter, school holidays).

Flight Duration: Australia is a large country, so flight times between cities can range from 1 to 6 hours. For example, flights between Sydney and Melbourne take about 1.5 hours, while flights from Sydney to Perth take around 4 hours.

Airports:

Major Hubs: Sydney (SYD), Melbourne (MEL), Brisbane (BNE), Perth (PER), and Adelaide (ADL) are the largest airports with international and domestic connections.

Regional Airports: Smaller airports in cities like Cairns, Hobart, and Alice Springs offer connections to regional destinations.

Luggage and Check-in:

Most airlines allow one checked bag (20-30 kg) and one carry-on bag (7-10 kg). Be mindful of baggage limits to avoid extra charges.

Arrive at the airport at least 1.5 to 2 hours before your flight for domestic check-in and security.

2. Ferries

Ferries are a fantastic way to explore Australia's coastal regions, island destinations, and nearby cities. Ferries offer a scenic and leisurely travel option, and in some cases, they are the only way to access certain destinations.

Popular Ferry Routes:

Sydney Harbour Ferries: One of the most iconic ferry experiences, providing spectacular views of Sydney Opera House, Harbour Bridge, and waterfront suburbs like Manly, Watsons Bay, and Taronga Zoo.

Ferry to Tasmania: The **Spirit of Tasmania** ferry travels from Melbourne to Devonport in Tasmania, offering a great way to arrive in this island state.

Ferries to Fraser Island: Ferries run from Hervey Bay and Rainbow Beach to Fraser Island, a UNESCO World Heritage site known for its diverse landscapes.

Great Barrier Reef Ferries: From Cairns and Port Douglas, ferries take you to the islands of the Great Barrier Reef, such as Green Island and Fitzroy Island.

Ferries to Kangaroo Island: Travel from the South Australian mainland to Kangaroo Island via ferry for wildlife encounters, hiking, and stunning beaches.

Booking and Schedules:

Ferry tickets can usually be purchased online or at the port. It's advisable to book in advance, especially during peak seasons.

Ferries may run on a set schedule, but availability can vary depending on the time of year, weather conditions, and route. Always check for any updates or cancellations.

What to Expect on a Ferry:

Ferries vary in size and comfort, from smaller boats to large vessels with cafes, restrooms, and seating areas.

On longer journeys (e.g., Spirit of Tasmania), cabins are available for overnight travel.

Some ferries offer scenic viewing decks, making them ideal for photo opportunities during the journey.

3. Travel Tips for Domestic Flights and Ferries

Flying Tips:

Weather: Check the weather forecast as storms can cause flight delays or cancellations.

Airport Transfers: Plan ahead for airport transfers to and from your accommodation, especially in large cities.

Loyalty Programs: Many airlines offer frequent flyer programs that allow you to earn points for future flights and upgrades.

Ferry Tips:

Seasickness: If you're prone to seasickness, consider taking motion sickness medication before boarding, particularly on longer ferry rides.

What to Bring: Pack snacks, sunscreen, and a hat if you're planning to spend time outside on the deck.

Accessibility: Most ferries are wheelchair accessible, but it's recommended to inform the ferry company in advance if you need special assistance.

4. Costs

Domestic Flights:

Flight prices vary depending on the distance, airline, and booking time. Flights between major cities typically cost between AUD $50 to $300, while regional flights can range from AUD $100 to $600.

Ferries:

Ferry fares vary depending on the route. Short ferry rides (like those around Sydney) cost around AUD $10-$20 one way, while longer ferries (like to Tasmania) may cost between AUD $100-$200 for a single passenger, with additional costs for vehicles or cabins.

Cycling and Walking

Cycling in Australia

Cycling is a popular way to explore the country's diverse landscapes, from urban cityscapes to remote national parks. Many cities have well-developed bike infrastructure, and there are numerous scenic cycling routes across the country.

Popular Cycling Routes:

Great Ocean Road (Victoria): One of the world's most scenic cycling routes, this path follows the southern coastline, offering stunning views of cliffs, beaches, and the Twelve Apostles.

Murray to Mountains Rail Trail (Victoria): This 100km trail offers a leisurely ride through Victoria's countryside, passing vineyards, quaint towns, and scenic rivers.

Tasmania's East Coast Cycling Loop: Explore Tasmania's natural beauty, from secluded beaches to lush forests, with this picturesque loop.

Brisbane's River Loop: A relaxing ride through Brisbane's urban core, following the river and passing through parks, cafes, and cultural spots.

Sydney to Manly Coastal Ride (New South Wales): A popular route that takes you from Sydney's Opera House to the beaches of Manly, passing through beautiful coastal parks and picturesque neighborhoods.

Cycling Tips:

Bike Rental: Most cities have bike rental stations, and services like **oBike** and **Lime** make it easy to pick up a bike for short trips.

Safety: Wear a helmet (mandatory in most places), use reflective gear for visibility, and make sure your bike is in good working condition.

Road Rules: Cyclists must follow the same road rules as drivers, including obeying traffic signals, riding in bike lanes, and using hand signals to indicate turns.

Walking in Australia

Walking is one of the best ways to take in Australia's natural beauty and unique urban environments. With a variety of landscapes, from lush rainforests to arid outback deserts, there's a walk for every kind of adventurer.

Popular Walking Trails:

The Overland Track (Tasmania): A world-famous 65-kilometer trail through the heart of Tasmania's wilderness, showcasing alpine meadows, rainforests, and dramatic landscapes.

The Larapinta Trail (Northern Territory): A challenging but rewarding 223-kilometer trek through the West MacDonnell Ranges, offering a true outback adventure.

The Blue Mountains (New South Wales): Known for its rugged terrain, the Blue Mountains feature a range of walking trails, from easy walks to more challenging treks, such as the **Grand Canyon Walk**.

Wilson's Promontory (Victoria): A coastal walk offering breathtaking views of beaches, cliffs, and diverse wildlife.

Kakadu National Park (Northern Territory): With its cultural significance and diverse landscapes, Kakadu offers a range of walks, from short strolls to multi-day hikes.

City Walking Tours:

Melbourne: Discover hidden laneways, street art, and cafes on foot. Melbourne is a walkable city with vibrant cultural precincts and historic buildings.

Sydney: Walk along the iconic **Bondi to Coogee Coastal Walk**, or explore the vibrant neighborhoods of The Rocks and Darling Harbour.

Adelaide: A great city for walking, offering parks, markets, and well-planned pedestrian paths.

Walking Tips:

Hydration and Protection: Australia's weather can be hot and sunny, so always carry water, sunscreen, and wear a hat to protect yourself from the sun.

Know Your Limits: Some walks, especially in remote areas, can be challenging and may require a reasonable level of fitness. Make sure to research the trail difficulty and plan accordingly.

Safety: In remote areas, be mindful of wildlife. Avoid walking alone in unfamiliar places, and let someone know your plans if venturing into the wilderness.

Accessible Cycling and Walking

Many parts of Australia offer accessible walking and cycling routes for those with limited mobility, including:

Wheelchair-friendly walks in places like **Royal Botanic Gardens** in Sydney and **Kings Park** in Perth.

Adaptive bike rental programs available in several cities, making cycling accessible to those with disabilities.

Chapter 3: Accommodation Options
Hotels and Resorts
Luxury Hotel

Luxury hotels in Australia offer an exceptional experience for travelers seeking comfort, elegance, and top-notch service. From stunning beachfront resorts to city-center retreats, these hotels provide world-class amenities, fine dining, and a range of exclusive services, ensuring a memorable and indulgent stay. Whether you're exploring the Great Barrier Reef, Sydney's iconic landmarks, or Melbourne's vibrant culture, luxury accommodations promise a perfect blend of relaxation and luxury for every traveler.

1. **Emirates One&Only Wolgan Valley, New South Wales**

Emirates One&Only Wolgan Valley is a luxurious eco-resort nestled in the stunning Blue Mountains. This all-inclusive resort offers privacy, comfort, and exceptional wildlife experiences, making it ideal for nature lovers and those seeking a serene escape.

Location:

Address: Wolgan Valley Road, Newnes, NSW, 2790, Australia

Proximity: Located 2.5 hours from Sydney, the resort is surrounded by more than 7,000 acres of conservation land.

Highlights:

- Secluded luxury villas with private pools
- Wildlife encounters, including kangaroo sightings and birdwatching
- Luxurious dining with locally sourced ingredients

Spa and Wellness:

One&Only Spa offers a range of treatments, including signature wellness therapies inspired by nature.

Fitness center and outdoor activities like hiking and horseback riding.

Bars:

The Wolgan Bar provides a cozy atmosphere with a selection of local wines and cocktails.

Events and Conferences:

Ideal for corporate retreats and small events.

Tailored conference packages available with state-of-the-art facilities.

Basic Facilities and Amenities:

- Infinity pool
- Private dining options
- Guided nature walks
- On-site boutique
- Library and games room

Opening and Closing Hours:

Check-in: 3:00 PM

Check-out: 11:00 AM

Price:
Starting from AUD $2,000 per night (all-inclusive).

Pros:

- Stunning natural setting
- All-inclusive experience
- Exclusive and private atmosphere

Cons:

- Price may be out of reach for some
- Remote location, requiring a long drive

Local Tips:

Book early for a chance to experience guided nature safaris.

Consider a helicopter transfer for an extra luxurious experience.

2. The Langham, Sydney

The Langham Sydney blends classical elegance with modern luxury. Located in the historic Rocks district, this hotel provides easy access to iconic attractions like the Sydney Opera House and Harbour Bridge.

Location:
Address: 89-113 Kent Street, Sydney, NSW 2000, Australia

Proximity: A short walk from Circular Quay and Sydney's main attractions.

Highlights:

- Panoramic views of Sydney Harbour
- Exceptional dining at Kitchens on Kent
- Iconic Afternoon Tea service

Spa and Wellness:

Chuan Spa offers traditional Chinese medicine-inspired treatments.

A fully equipped gym and indoor swimming pool.

Bars:

The Bar at The Langham serves signature cocktails and a fine selection of wines.

Events and Conferences:

Offers 14 event spaces, perfect for conferences and weddings.

State-of-the-art audiovisual equipment.

Basic Facilities and Amenities:

- Indoor pool
- Full-service business center
- Luxury concierge service
- Babysitting services available

Opening and Closing Hours:

Check-in: 3:00 PM

Check-out: 12:00 PM

Price:
Starting from AUD $450 per night.

Pros:

- Close to major attractions
- Exceptional dining and spa services
- Elegant and refined atmosphere

Cons:

- Can be expensive for long stays
- Limited views from some rooms

Local Tips:

Visit the nearby Barangaroo for trendy restaurants and views of the harbor.

Take a short walk to the historic Rocks Markets on weekends.

3. Sofitel Sydney Darling Harbour

Sofitel Sydney Darling Harbour combines contemporary design with French-inspired elegance, offering a luxurious stay with stunning views of Darling Harbour.

Location:
Address: 12 Darling Drive, Darling Harbour, Sydney, NSW 2000, Australia
Proximity: Just a 5-minute walk to the Sydney Aquarium and Star Casino.

Highlights:

- Spectacular views of Darling Harbour
- 35-meter infinity pool with views over the water
- Vibrant rooftop bar with signature cocktails

Spa and Wellness:

SoFit fitness center, an indoor lap pool, and wellness services.

In-room spa treatments upon request.

Bars:

SoBar, a stylish rooftop bar with panoramic city views.

Events and Conferences:

Offers flexible meeting rooms with modern amenities.

Event spaces can host up to 600 people.

Basic Facilities and Amenities:

- 24-hour concierge service
- Business center and meeting rooms
- High-speed internet
- Pet-friendly accommodations

Opening and Closing Hours:

Check-in: 3:00 PM

Check-out: 12:00 PM

Price:
Starting from AUD $350 per night.

Pros:

- Modern and stylish design
- Ideal for business and leisure travelers
- Great location for exploring the city

Cons:

- Higher-end rooms can be quite pricey
- The area can be busy and crowded, especially during peak season

Local Tips:

Take a sunset walk along the Darling Harbour promenade.

Explore the nearby Cockle Bay Wharf for dining and shopping options.

4. Qualia, Hamilton Island

Qualia is an exclusive resort located on Hamilton Island, part of the Whitsunday Islands, offering five-star service and access to the Great Barrier Reef.

Location:

Address: Whitsunday Islands, Hamilton Island, Queensland 4803, Australia
Proximity: A short 1-hour flight from Brisbane or Cairns, with direct transfers from the airport to the resort.

Highlights:

- Private beachfront location
- Stunning views of the Coral Sea
- Award-winning dining options

Spa and Wellness:

Spa Qualia offers a range of luxury treatments, from facials to massages.

Yoga and wellness programs are available.

Bars:

Long Pavilion Bar provides tropical cocktails with ocean views.

Events and Conferences:

Perfect for destination weddings and small corporate events.

Private venues with stunning views of the sea.

Basic Facilities and Amenities:

- Private plunge pools in select rooms
- Beachfront access
- Water sports activities
- Luxury concierge services

Opening and Closing Hours:

Check-in: 3:00 PM

Check-out: 11:00 AM

Price:
Starting from AUD $1,500 per night.

Pros:

- Stunning location with direct access to the Great Barrier Reef
- Intimate, tranquil atmosphere
- Exceptional service

Cons:

- Price is on the higher end
- Remote location may not appeal to all

Local Tips:

Don't miss a day trip to the Great Barrier Reef.

Book a private dining experience on the beach for a unique experience.

5. Palazzo Versace, Gold Coast

Palazzo Versace offers a lavish stay with a blend of Italian luxury and coastal charm. This fashion-inspired hotel is located on the Gold Coast and provides an upscale experience for those looking for the ultimate in style and elegance.

Location:
Address: 94 Seaworld Drive, Main Beach, Gold Coast, QLD 4217, Australia
Proximity: 5-minute drive from Surfers Paradise and major theme parks.

Highlights:

- Iconic design with Versace furnishings
- Private marina and yacht services
- 2 gourmet restaurants

Spa and Wellness:

Versace Spa offers indulgent treatments, including massages and facials.

Fitness center and outdoor pool.

Bars:

La Medusa Bar, offering cocktails and light bites in a luxurious setting.

Events and Conferences:

Versace Ballroom is ideal for large conferences and weddings.

Customizable packages for corporate events.

Basic Facilities and Amenities:

- Private beach access
- 24-hour room service
- Valet parking
- Luxury shopping boutiques

Opening and Closing Hours:

Check-in: 3:00 PM

Check-out: 11:00 AM

Price:
Starting from AUD $550 per night.

Pros:

- Luxurious and unique interior design
- Great location for beach lovers
- High-end facilities and services

Cons:

- Can be expensive for long stays
- Some may find the opulent style too over-the-top

Local Tips:

Take a short drive to the theme parks or visit the nearby Broadwater Parklands.

Explore the local dining scene at the Marina Mirage.

Mid-Range Hotel

Mid-range hotels in Australia offer a comfortable and affordable stay without compromising on quality. These hotels provide convenient locations, essential amenities, and a relaxing atmosphere for travelers seeking a balance between luxury and budget-friendly options. Whether you're exploring vibrant cities, coastal regions, or scenic landscapes, mid-range hotels offer a great choice for a pleasant and hassle-free vacation experience.

1. The Rendezvous Hotel, Melbourne

The Rendezvous Hotel Melbourne offers stylish and contemporary accommodations in the heart of the city. Its historical architecture blends with modern amenities, making it a great choice for travelers seeking comfort and convenience.

Location:

Address: 328 Flinders Street, Melbourne, VIC 3000, Australia

Proximity: Centrally located near Federation Square, Flinders Street Station, and the National Gallery of Victoria.

Highlights:

- Central location for sightseeing and shopping
- Beautiful heritage building with a mix of modern rooms
- Walking distance to Melbourne's top attractions

Spa and Wellness:

No on-site spa, but wellness services are available upon request.

Fitness center with basic equipment.

Bars:

The Rendezvous Bar offers cocktails and light snacks in a relaxed setting.

Events and Conferences:

Several event spaces suitable for small to mid-sized meetings and conferences.

Event staff and technical support available.

Basic Facilities and Amenities:

- Free Wi-Fi
- Room service
- Concierge services
- Business center

Opening and Closing Hours:

Check-in: 2:00 PM

Check-out: 10:00 AM

Price:
Starting from AUD $160 per night.

Pros:

- Great central location
- Affordable prices for the quality and location
- Comfortable rooms

Cons:

- Rooms can be a bit small
- Limited dining options on-site

Local Tips:

Visit the nearby Hosier Lane for unique street art and local cafes.

Take a short walk to the Melbourne Museum and Royal Exhibition Building.

2. Mantra on Kent, Sydney

Mantra on Kent is a well-rated mid-range hotel offering spacious accommodations in a prime location. Perfect for those visiting Sydney for business or leisure, it provides a welcoming atmosphere with excellent service.

Location:
Address: 433 Kent Street, Sydney, NSW 2000, Australia

Proximity: Located near Darling Harbour and a short walk to the Queen Victoria Building and Pitt Street Mall.

Highlights:

- Spacious apartments with kitchenettes
- Easy access to public transport and local attractions
- Close to entertainment and shopping areas

Spa and Wellness:

On-site heated indoor pool and fitness center.

No dedicated spa, but wellness treatments can be arranged upon request.

Bars:

No dedicated bar, but there are several nearby bars and restaurants.

Events and Conferences:

Meeting and event spaces available for small conferences.

Business facilities, including internet and office equipment.

Basic Facilities and Amenities:

- Free Wi-Fi
- 24-hour reception
- In-room laundry facilities
- On-site parking (fee applies)

Opening and Closing Hours:

Check-in: 2:00 PM

Check-out: 10:00 AM

Price:
Starting from AUD $180 per night.

Pros:

- Spacious and well-equipped rooms
- Convenient location close to public transport
- Good value for money

Cons:

- No on-site restaurant or bar
- Limited room service options

Local Tips:

Take the ferry from Darling Harbour for a scenic view of Sydney's harbor.

Explore the nearby Pyrmont Bridge and the Star Casino for entertainment.

3. Peppers Blue on Blue, Magnetic Island

Peppers Blue on Blue is a serene mid-range resort located on Magnetic Island, offering a tropical getaway with stunning views and access to beautiful beaches.

Location:
Address: 123 Sooning Street, Nelly Bay, Magnetic Island, QLD 4819, Australia
Proximity: A short ferry ride from Townsville, the resort is close to Nelly Bay Beach and local attractions.

Highlights:

- Stunning views of the Coral Sea
- Large lagoon-style pool
- Close proximity to local beaches and nature walks

Spa and Wellness:

No dedicated spa, but wellness and relaxation services are available.

Poolside massage services offered.

Bars:

The Blue on Blue Restaurant & Bar offers cocktails and casual dining with scenic views.

Events and Conferences:

Conference facilities for small to medium-sized events.

Business support services available upon request.

Basic Facilities and Amenities:

- Free Wi-Fi
- Room service
- Fitness center
- On-site restaurant and bar

Opening and Closing Hours:

Check-in: 2:00 PM

Check-out: 10:00 AM

Price:
Starting from AUD $220 per night.

Pros:

- Ideal for relaxation and nature lovers
- Beautiful beachfront location
- Great amenities for families

Cons:

- A bit isolated if you're looking for a more urban experience
- Higher price point compared to other mid-range options

Local Tips:

Explore the nearby hiking trails, such as the Forts Walk, for wildlife sightings.

Rent a car or scooter to explore the island more freely.

4. The Sebel Melbourne Docklands

Overview:
The Sebel Melbourne Docklands offers a stylish, modern stay for guests looking to experience Melbourne's waterfront. With a range of amenities and close proximity to the city, it's perfect for both business and leisure travelers.

Location:
Address: 18 Aquitania Way, Docklands, VIC 3008, Australia

Proximity: Located along the Yarra River and only a short tram ride to Melbourne's central business district.

Highlights:

- Modern, spacious rooms with city or water views
- Walking distance to Marvel Stadium and Etihad Stadium
- Close to shopping precincts and restaurants

Spa and Wellness:

- On-site fitness center and swimming pool.
- No dedicated spa, but wellness treatments available on request.

Bars:

On-site bar and lounge area, ideal for a relaxed evening with drinks.

Events and Conferences:

Conference and meeting rooms available for business events.

Full event support and high-tech facilities.

Basic Facilities and Amenities:

- Free Wi-Fi
- 24-hour reception
- Kitchenettes in rooms
- Room service

Opening and Closing Hours:

Check-in: 2:00 PM

Check-out: 10:00 AM

Price:
Starting from AUD $190 per night.

Pros:

- Modern amenities and stylish interiors
- Ideal for business travelers and families

Waterfront location with easy access to city attractions

Cons:

Can be noisy due to its proximity to sports events

Parking charges apply

Local Tips:

Take a walk along the Docklands Promenade for beautiful views of the marina.

Try the nearby Docklands Park for outdoor activities and relaxation.

5. Mercure Brisbane

Mercure Brisbane offers a great mid-range option with contemporary design and a central location. It's ideal for tourists who want to explore Brisbane while enjoying comfortable accommodations and modern amenities.

Location:
Address: 85-87 North Quay, Brisbane, QLD 4000, Australia

Proximity: Located near the Brisbane River, the hotel is close to Queen Street Mall, South Bank, and the Brisbane Convention Centre.

Highlights:

- Central location in Brisbane's vibrant CBD
- Rooftop pool with panoramic views
- Proximity to local attractions, shopping, and dining options

Spa and Wellness:

Fitness center and rooftop pool.

No dedicated spa, but wellness services are available upon request.

Bars:

No dedicated bar, but the hotel offers room service and the option to enjoy drinks in the lounge area.

Events and Conferences:

Offers several meeting rooms and event spaces for conferences and events.

Full event services, including catering and audiovisual equipment.

Basic Facilities and Amenities:

- Free Wi-Fi
- 24-hour reception
- Concierge services
- Business center

Opening and Closing Hours:

Check-in: 2:00 PM

Check-out: 11:00 AM

Price:
Starting from AUD $170 per night.

Pros:

- Excellent location for city exploration
- Great value for the price
- Modern amenities and friendly staff

Cons:

- Limited dining options on-site
- Can get busy during peak tourist seasons

Local Tips:

Visit South Bank Parklands for great outdoor activities and dining.

Take a ferry ride along the Brisbane River for scenic views of the city.

Hostels and Budget Stays

Hostels

Hostels in Australia offer budget-friendly accommodations for travelers looking for a simple and social place to stay. With shared dorms and private rooms, hostels provide a great option for those wanting to meet other travelers and explore the country without breaking the bank. Conveniently located in major cities and tourist spots, hostels offer essential amenities like free Wi-Fi, communal kitchens, and organized activities, making them perfect for those seeking affordability and a vibrant atmosphere.

1. Wake Up! Sydney Central, Sydney

Wake Up! Sydney Central is a lively and modern hostel located in the heart of Sydney. Known for its vibrant atmosphere, this hostel attracts solo travelers, backpackers, and groups looking to meet new people while staying close to iconic attractions like the Sydney Opera House and Darling Harbour.

Location:
Address: 509 Pitt Street, Sydney, NSW 2000, Australia

Proximity: 10-minute walk to Central Station, a short walk to the famous Sydney attractions.

Highlights:

- Modern, stylish design with a range of room options
- Proximity to public transport and major sights
- Regular social events and tours organized by the hostel

Spa and Wellness:

No dedicated spa, but offers a fitness room for guests.

Wellness activities available on request.

Bars:

The Rooftop Bar serves drinks and has great views of the city skyline.

Events and Conferences:

Hosts social events, such as trivia nights, BBQs, and pub crawls, for guests to meet and interact.

Basic Facilities and Amenities:

- Free Wi-Fi
- Kitchen facilities
- 24-hour reception
- Laundry facilities

Opening and Closing Hours:

Check-in: 2:00 PM

Check-out: 10:00 AM

Price:
Starting from AUD $30 per night for dorms.

Pros:

- Central location with easy access to transport
- Fun and social atmosphere
- Clean and modern facilities

Cons:

- Can get noisy due to the lively environment
- Not ideal for those looking for a quiet stay

Local Tips:

Take a short walk to visit the nearby Chinatown for affordable food options.

Join the hostel's guided city tour to discover hidden gems in Sydney.

2. **The Village Bondi Beach, Sydney**

The Village Bondi Beach is a relaxed and friendly hostel located just minutes from Bondi Beach. This hostel is perfect for beach lovers and those who want to enjoy Sydney's laid-back vibe while staying close to the beach.

Location:
Address: 19-23 Lamrock Avenue, Bondi Beach, NSW 2026, Australia
Proximity: Just a 5-minute walk to Bondi Beach and 15 minutes from Bondi Junction.

Highlights:

- Close proximity to the world-famous Bondi Beach
- Beachside activities and relaxed environment
- Spacious and clean dorms and private rooms

Spa and Wellness:

No on-site spa, but offers access to nearby wellness centers.

Surfboard rentals available for guests.

Bars:

On-site bar with a casual vibe, perfect for post-beach relaxation.

Events and Conferences:

Regular social events, including movie nights, BBQs, and pub crawls.

Basic Facilities and Amenities:

- Free Wi-Fi
- Fully equipped kitchen
- Laundry facilities
- Communal lounge area

Opening and Closing Hours:

Check-in: 2:00 PM

Check-out: 10:00 AM

Price:
Starting from AUD $35 per night for dorm rooms.

Pros:

- Ideal location for beach lovers

- Social atmosphere with friendly staff
- Clean and well-maintained facilities

Cons:

- Can be crowded during peak season
- Limited privacy in shared dorms

Local Tips:

Take the Bondi to Coogee coastal walk for stunning ocean views.

Grab a bite at one of the many beachfront cafes around Bondi.

3. Nomads Brisbane, Brisbane

Nomads Brisbane is a fun, social hostel located near Brisbane's Central Business District. It offers affordable accommodations with a mix of modern amenities and social activities for backpackers and tourists looking to explore the city.

Location:

Address: 308 Edward Street, Brisbane, QLD 4000, Australia

Proximity: Close to Queen Street Mall, South Bank, and the Brisbane River.

Highlights:

Central location with easy access to public transport

Regular activities, including free walking tours and karaoke nights

On-site cafe for quick bites

Spa and Wellness:

No on-site spa, but guests can use local gyms with discounted passes.

Yoga and fitness sessions available in the area.

Bars:

The Down Under Bar serves drinks and hosts themed events.

Events and Conferences:

Regular social events, including live music and parties, making it a great place to meet other travelers.

Basic Facilities and Amenities:

- Free Wi-Fi
- Kitchen facilities
- Laundry services
- 24-hour reception

Opening and Closing Hours:

Check-in: 2:00 PM

Check-out: 10:00 AM

Price:
Starting from AUD $25 per night for dorms.

Pros:

- Central city location
- Plenty of social activities and opportunities to meet other travelers
- Clean and comfortable rooms

Cons:

Can be noisy at times due to the social atmosphere

Limited privacy in shared dorm rooms

Local Tips:

Explore Brisbane's South Bank for outdoor markets, gardens, and restaurants.

Take the ferry across the Brisbane River to see the city from a different angle.

4. Backpackers HQ, Melbourne

Backpackers HQ is a well-established hostel in Melbourne, offering budget accommodations in a prime location. Known for its friendly and welcoming environment, it's a great spot for travelers who want to explore the cultural capital of Australia.

Location:

Address: 22 Little Collins Street, Melbourne, VIC 3000, Australia Proximity: Located in the heart of Melbourne's Central Business District, near Federation Square and Flinders Street Station.

Highlights:

Ideal location for accessing Melbourne's shopping, dining, and cultural attractions

Great value for money

Cozy and communal atmosphere

Spa and Wellness:

No dedicated spa, but nearby wellness centers offer discounted treatments for guests.

Fitness center access available with a guest pass.

Bars:

Bar located on-site for casual drinks and socializing.

Events and Conferences:

Regular movie nights, pub crawls, and social mixers.

Basic Facilities and Amenities:

Free Wi-Fi

Fully equipped kitchen

Laundry facilities

Communal lounge area

Opening and Closing Hours:

Check-in: 2:00 PM

Check-out: 10:00 AM

Price:
Starting from AUD $28 per night for dorms.

Pros:

- Excellent central location
- Affordable and good value for money
- Friendly staff and social environment

Cons:

- Rooms can be basic and compact
- Limited privacy in shared spaces

Local Tips:

Visit Melbourne's laneways for unique street art and hidden cafes.

Take a tram to St Kilda Beach for a relaxing day by the sea.

5. YHA Cairns Central, Cairns

Overview:
YHA Cairns Central is a well-regarded hostel that offers a relaxing base for travelers visiting Far North Queensland. Located in the heart of Cairns, it's ideal for those looking to explore the Great Barrier Reef and other nearby natural attractions.

Location:
Address: 20-26 McLeod Street, Cairns, QLD 4870, Australia

Proximity: Just a short walk to the Esplanade and the Cairns Lagoon.

Highlights:

Prime location close to the Great Barrier Reef departure points

Comfortable, air-conditioned rooms

Close to local shops, restaurants, and cafes

Spa and Wellness:

No on-site spa, but access to local wellness services and gyms is available.

Bars:

On-site bar serving casual drinks and snacks.

Events and Conferences:

Social events organized regularly, including BBQs and trivia nights.

Basic Facilities and Amenities:

Free Wi-Fi

Fully equipped kitchen

Laundry facilities

Tour desk for booking excursions

Opening and Closing Hours:

Check-in: 2:00 PM

Check-out: 10:00 AM

Price:
Starting from AUD $24 per night for dorm rooms.

Pros:

- Great location near the Esplanade and lagoon
- Affordable and clean
- Friendly and social atmosphere

Cons:

- Can be busy during peak tourist seasons
- Limited privacy in shared dorms

Local Tips:

Book your Great Barrier Reef tours early to secure the best spots.

Visit the Cairns Night Markets for unique souvenirs and local food.

Budget Stays

Budget stays in Australia provide affordable and practical accommodation options for travelers looking to explore the country without spending too much. These options include hostels, guesthouses, and budget hotels, offering basic amenities, comfortable rooms, and convenient locations. Perfect for those on a tight budget, budget stays ensure a simple and stress-free base to enjoy all that Australia has to offer.

1. The Pod Sydney, Sydney

The Pod Sydney is a budget-friendly, boutique hostel offering compact, capsule-style pods for a more private experience in a lively, social environment. Perfect for solo travelers and those on a budget who want to stay in the heart of Sydney.

Location:
Address: 396 Pitt Street, Haymarket, Sydney, NSW 2000, Australia

Proximity: Located near Central Station, close to Chinatown and a short walk from Darling Harbour and other attractions.

Highlights:

- Private pods for added comfort and privacy
- Central location with easy access to public transport
- Modern, stylish interior design

Spa and Wellness:

No dedicated spa, but wellness treatments can be arranged nearby.

Bars:

On-site bar with a chill atmosphere for meeting fellow travelers.

Events and Conferences:

Regular social events like pub crawls and movie nights for guests.

Basic Facilities and Amenities:

- Free Wi-Fi

- Kitchen facilities
- Lockers for personal belongings
- 24-hour reception

Opening and Closing Hours:

Check-in: 2:00 PM

Check-out: 10:00 AM

Price:
Starting from AUD $40 per night for dorm rooms.

Pros:

- Great location for exploring Sydney
- Private and secure pods
- Budget-friendly option with good facilities

Cons:

- Limited space in pods
- Can get noisy during peak times

Local Tips:

Explore nearby Chinatown for affordable meals.

Take a walk through nearby Hyde Park to enjoy some green space in the city.

2. **YHA Melbourne Central, Melbourne**

YHA Melbourne Central is a well-located, budget-friendly hostel offering clean and comfortable accommodations in the heart of Melbourne. Known for its welcoming atmosphere and social events, it's perfect for young travelers.

Location:
Address: 392 Little Bourke Street, Melbourne, VIC 3000, Australia

Proximity: Close to Melbourne's top attractions like Federation Square, Queen Victoria Market, and the Melbourne Museum.

Highlights:

- Central location near shops, cafes, and tourist spots
- Clean and modern rooms with both shared and private options
- Eco-friendly practices and sustainability efforts

Spa and Wellness:

No spa services, but wellness centers are available nearby.

Bars:

No on-site bar, but a communal lounge area for guests to socialize.

Events and Conferences:

Offers events like city tours, movie nights, and free walking tours for guests.

Basic Facilities and Amenities:

- Free Wi-Fi
- Kitchen facilities
- Laundry services
- 24-hour reception

Opening and Closing Hours:

Check-in: 2:00 PM

Check-out: 10:00 AM

Price:
Starting from AUD $30 per night for dorm rooms.

Pros:

- Great central location
- Friendly, social atmosphere
- Affordable and clean accommodations

Cons:

Shared bathrooms may be less convenient during peak hours

No dedicated bar on-site

Local Tips:

Visit the Queen Victoria Market for fresh food and unique souvenirs.

Take a walk to the rooftop for a great view of the city.

3. Base Backpackers, Brisbane

Base Backpackers in Brisbane offers affordable dorm-style rooms and a friendly, social atmosphere, perfect for budget travelers looking to explore the city. It's located in a central spot, with plenty of nearby attractions.

Location:
Address: 308 Edward Street, Brisbane, QLD 4000, Australia

Proximity: Close to the Queen Street Mall, South Bank Parklands, and public transport options.

Highlights:

- Central location with easy access to key attractions
- Regular social events to help guests connect
- Clean, comfortable dorms with air conditioning

Spa and Wellness:

No on-site spa, but gyms and wellness centers are available nearby.

Bars:

The Base Bar offers a relaxed atmosphere for drinks and meeting new people.

Events and Conferences:

Hosts events like karaoke nights, BBQs, and walking tours.

Basic Facilities and Amenities:

- Free Wi-Fi
- Kitchen facilities
- Laundry facilities
- 24-hour reception

Opening and Closing Hours:

Check-in: 2:00 PM

Check-out: 10:00 AM

Price:
Starting from AUD $25 per night for dorms.

Pros:

- Great social atmosphere with regular events
- Prime location close to attractions and public transport
- Affordable rates

Cons:

- Can be noisy due to social activities
- Shared bathrooms can get busy

Local Tips:

Head to South Bank for a day by the river and a visit to the Gallery of Modern Art.

Check out the local markets for fresh produce and local goods.

4. Kangaroo Hostel, Melbourne

Kangaroo Hostel offers a budget-friendly, no-frills stay in the heart of Melbourne. It's a popular choice for backpackers looking for affordable and comfortable accommodations with easy access to the city's attractions.

Location:
Address: 161-163 Barkly Street, St Kilda, Melbourne, VIC 3182, Australia
Proximity: Close to St Kilda Beach and just a short tram ride from Melbourne's city center.

Highlights:

- Affordable, basic accommodation with a social vibe
- Close to the beach and Melbourne's vibrant nightlife
- Offers both dorm rooms and private rooms

Spa and Wellness:

No spa services, but nearby wellness options are available.

Bars:

On-site bar for guests to enjoy drinks and socialize.

Events and Conferences:

Hosts regular social events, pub crawls, and BBQ nights.

Basic Facilities and Amenities:

- Free Wi-Fi
- Kitchen and BBQ facilities
- Laundry facilities
- 24-hour reception

Opening and Closing Hours:

Check-in: 2:00 PM

Check-out: 10:00 AM

Price:
Starting from AUD $28 per night for dorm rooms.

Pros:

- Close to the beach and nightlife
- Good for budget-conscious travelers
- Regular social events

Cons:

- Can be noisy due to social activities
- Shared bathrooms may be inconvenient during busy periods

Local Tips:

Visit the St Kilda Pier for a beautiful sunset view.

Take the tram to Melbourne's city center for shopping and dining.

5. The Mad Monkey Backpackers, Cairns

The Mad Monkey Backpackers in Cairns is a laid-back, budget-friendly option that offers a social atmosphere for travelers exploring Far North Queensland. Known for its welcoming vibe and friendly staff, it's perfect for those looking to relax and socialize.

Location:

Address: 87 Grafton Street, Cairns, QLD 4870, Australia

Proximity: Walking distance to the Esplanade, local markets, and public transport.

Highlights:

- Social and relaxed atmosphere with a pool
- Close proximity to Cairns' top attractions, including the Great Barrier Reef
- Offers both dormitory and private room options

Spa and Wellness:

No on-site spa, but wellness centers and massage services are available in Cairns.

Bars:

On-site bar for drinks and a laid-back atmosphere.

Events and Conferences:

Regular events like BBQs, pub crawls, and dive trips.

Basic Facilities and Amenities:

- Free Wi-Fi
- Kitchen facilities
- Laundry services
- Swimming pool

Opening and Closing Hours:

Check-in: 2:00 PM

Check-out: 10:00 AM

Price:

Starting from AUD $22 per night for dorm rooms.

Pros:

Great social vibe with plenty of events

Budget-friendly

Central location with easy access to the Great Barrier Reef

Cons:

Can be noisy due to the social atmosphere

Shared bathrooms can get crowded during peak times

Local Tips:

Take a day trip to the Great Barrier Reef or explore nearby rainforest hikes.

Visit the Cairns Night Markets for souvenirs and local food.

Airbnb and Vacation Rentals

Airbnb and vacation rentals offer a home-like experience for travelers seeking more privacy and flexibility during their stay in Australia. These accommodations range from entire homes and apartments to unique properties like beach houses or rural retreats. Perfect for families, groups, or those seeking a more personalized experience, Airbnb and vacation rentals provide comfort, convenience, and the opportunity to live like a local while exploring the country.

1. The Beach House, Byron Bay (Airbnb)

The Beach House in Byron Bay offers a luxurious, private escape just steps from the famous beaches. This spacious home provides the perfect balance of modern amenities and tropical beach vibes, ideal for families or groups.

Location:
Address: 3/6 Carlyle Street, Byron Bay, NSW 2481, Australia

Proximity: A 5-minute walk to the beach and close to Byron Bay's vibrant town center.

Highlights:

- Modern beach house with a large outdoor deck
- Private pool and lush tropical garden
- Close proximity to the beach and town center

Spa and Wellness:

Private outdoor jacuzzi

Nearby wellness centers and yoga studios for relaxation and rejuvenation.

Bars:

No on-site bar, but nearby Byron Bay has numerous bars and cafes.

Events and Conferences:

Not specifically geared for large events, but ideal for small gatherings and family vacations.

Basic Facilities and Amenities:

- Free Wi-Fi
- Fully equipped kitchen
- Private pool and jacuzzi
- Air conditioning and heating

Opening and Closing Hours:

Flexible check-in/check-out times, typically after 2:00 PM and by 10:00 AM.

Price:
Starting from AUD $400 per night.

Pros:

- Close to the beach and town center
- Private, luxurious experience
- Spacious and comfortable for large groups

Cons:

- Higher price point, especially during peak seasons
- No direct access to a bar or restaurant

Local Tips:

Don't miss the sunrise at Byron Bay Lighthouse for incredible views.

Explore the local farmers' markets for fresh, local produce.

2. **Luxury Penthouse, Sydney (Airbnb)**

This luxury penthouse offers a stunning view of Sydney's skyline and harbor. With high-end finishes and a prime location, it's perfect for those wanting a taste of luxury in the heart of the city.

Location:
Address: 72 Pyrmont Bridge Road, Pyrmont, Sydney, NSW 2009, Australia
Proximity: Close to Darling Harbour, the Sydney Opera House, and the Rocks area.

Highlights:

- Panoramic views of the Sydney Opera House and Harbor Bridge
- Spacious rooftop terrace
- Stylish interior with luxurious furnishings

Spa and Wellness:

No on-site spa, but the area is home to several wellness spas and fitness centers.

Bars:

Roof-top bar for evening drinks with a view.

Events and Conferences:

Ideal for small private events or corporate retreats, but not suited for large-scale conferences.

Basic Facilities and Amenities:

- Free Wi-Fi
- Fully equipped kitchen
- Air conditioning and heating
- Rooftop terrace and BBQ facilities

Opening and Closing Hours:

Flexible check-in/check-out times.

Price:
Starting from AUD $600 per night.

Pros:

- Stunning location with great views
- High-end amenities
- Ideal for luxury stays in the city

Cons:

- Expensive, particularly for longer stays
- Limited space for large groups

Local Tips:

Walk to the nearby Barangaroo Reserve for an incredible waterfront experience.

Take a ferry from Darling Harbour to Circular Quay for scenic views of the harbor.

3. Charming Cottage, Melbourne (Vacation Rental)

This charming cottage in Melbourne offers a cozy, homey atmosphere with easy access to the city's vibrant dining and shopping scene. Ideal for those seeking a quaint and quiet retreat with close proximity to the action.

Location:
Address: 38 Little Oxford Street, Melbourne, VIC 3000, Australia
Proximity: Close to Melbourne's central business district, Queen Victoria Market, and Carlton Gardens.

Highlights:

- Cozy, intimate cottage with rustic charm
- Private garden and outdoor seating area
- Central location for easy city exploration

Spa and Wellness:

No spa services, but there are several spas nearby in the city center.

Bars:

No on-site bar, but Melbourne is home to a fantastic bar scene with numerous options nearby.

Events and Conferences:

Not intended for large-scale events, but perfect for small gatherings or family holidays.

Basic Facilities and Amenities:

- Free Wi-Fi
- Kitchen facilities
- Laundry facilities
- Air conditioning and heating

Opening and Closing Hours:

Check-in: 3:00 PM

Check-out: 11:00 AM

Price:
Starting from AUD $180 per night.

Pros:

- Cozy and private space
- Quiet, yet close to the city's attractions
- Great for couples or small families

Cons:

- Smaller size, less suitable for large groups
- Limited amenities on-site

Local Tips:

Explore nearby Carlton for its famous Italian dining options.

Take a walk through the Royal Botanic Gardens for a peaceful escape from the city bustle.

4. Seaside Retreat, Gold Coast (Vacation Rental)

This beachfront retreat offers a relaxing escape with stunning views of the Pacific Ocean. Perfect for those who want to enjoy the beautiful beaches of the Gold Coast while staying in a stylish and comfortable space.

Location:
Address: 115 Marine Parade, Coolangatta, Gold Coast, QLD 4225, Australia
Proximity: Steps from Coolangatta Beach and just a short drive from major theme parks and Gold Coast attractions.

Highlights:

- Oceanfront views and easy beach access
- Large outdoor deck for relaxing or entertaining
- Modern, stylish interiors with beachy vibes

Spa and Wellness:

No spa on-site, but wellness retreats and spas are nearby.

Bars:

No on-site bar, but many beachfront cafes and bars nearby.

Events and Conferences:

Great for intimate gatherings or family events, but not suited for large conferences.

Basic Facilities and Amenities:

- Free Wi-Fi
- Kitchen facilities
- Outdoor BBQ area
- Air conditioning

Opening and Closing Hours:

Flexible check-in/check-out times.

Price:
Starting from AUD $350 per night.

Pros:

- Close proximity to the beach
- Modern and stylish accommodations
- Ideal for families or small groups

Cons:

- Can be pricey during peak season
- Not ideal for larger events or conferences

Local Tips:

Visit the nearby Currumbin Wildlife Sanctuary to see native animals up close.

Explore Coolangatta's cafes and surf spots for a laid-back vibe.

5. The Loft, Adelaide (Airbnb)

The Loft in Adelaide offers a modern and chic retreat right in the heart of the city. This stylish property is ideal for couples or solo travelers looking for a central location with contemporary comforts.

Location:

Address: 42 Grote Street, Adelaide, SA 5000, Australia

Proximity: Close to Rundle Mall, Adelaide Central Market, and the Adelaide Botanic Garden.

Highlights:

Trendy and modern loft-style apartment

Large windows with views of the city

Central location with easy access to shopping, dining, and culture

Spa and Wellness:

No on-site spa, but several wellness centers and spas are available in the area.

Bars:

No on-site bar, but Adelaide offers a vibrant nightlife scene with many bars nearby.

Events and Conferences:

Suitable for small meetings or events, but not large conferences.

Basic Facilities and Amenities:

- Free Wi-Fi
- Fully equipped kitchen
- Laundry facilities
- Air conditioning and heating

Opening and Closing Hours:

Flexible check-in/check-out times.

Price:
Starting from AUD $220 per night.

Pros:

- Central location in Adelaide
- Modern and stylish apartment
- Perfect for couples or solo travelers

Cons:

- Not suitable for larger groups
- Limited on-site amenities

Local Tips:

Check out the Adelaide Central Market for fresh food and local goods.

Walk to the Adelaide Hills for a scenic day trip.

Luxury and Eco-Friendly Lodging

Luxury and eco-friendly lodging in Australia offers a sustainable yet indulgent experience for travelers. These accommodations combine high-end comfort with eco-conscious practices, allowing guests to enjoy premium amenities while minimizing their environmental impact. Perfect for those seeking a balance between luxury and sustainability, these stays offer a unique opportunity to enjoy Australia's natural beauty responsibly.

1. **Emirates One&Only Wolgan Valley, New South Wales**

Emirates One&Only Wolgan Valley is a luxury eco-resort nestled in the Blue Mountains, surrounded by stunning natural landscapes. It blends luxury with sustainability, offering world-class service while preserving the environment.

Location:
Address: Wolgan Valley Road, Wolgan Valley, NSW 2790, Australia
Proximity: Located 2.5 hours from Sydney, the resort is in a secluded valley surrounded by a wildlife reserve.

Highlights:

Private luxury villas with panoramic views of the valley

Sustainable building practices using local materials

Extensive wildlife and nature experiences

Spa and Wellness:

Timeless Spa offering organic treatments and wellness programs

Yoga and meditation services available on request

Bars:

The Wolgan Bar offers a relaxing atmosphere with views of the valley.

Events and Conferences:

Suitable for small, intimate corporate retreats or weddings, with multiple event spaces available.

Basic Facilities and Amenities:

- Free Wi-Fi
- Heated swimming pool
- Private villa with fireplace
- Full-service dining options focusing on local, sustainable produce

Opening and Closing Hours:

Check-in: 3:00 PM

Check-out: 11:00 AM

Price:
Starting from AUD $2,300 per night (all-inclusive).

Pros:

- Secluded, luxurious experience in nature
- Focus on eco-friendly practices
- Ideal for relaxation and nature lovers

Cons:

- Expensive, especially during peak seasons
- Limited access to nearby towns

Local Tips:

Take a guided wildlife safari to explore the valley's diverse ecosystem.

Visit the nearby Wollemi National Park for hiking and scenic views.

2. Bamurru Plains, Northern Territory

Bamurru Plains is a luxury eco-lodge located in the Top End of the Northern Territory. Surrounded by wetlands, it offers an exclusive wildlife experience with a strong commitment to conservation.

Location:
Address: 1/214 Oolloo Road, Arnhem Land, Northern Territory 0822, Australia
Proximity: About 3 hours from Darwin, close to the Mary River wetlands.

Highlights:

Unique tented safari-style accommodations with views of the surrounding wetlands

Ideal for birdwatching and wildlife safaris

Built with eco-conscious materials and minimal environmental impact

Spa and Wellness:

Limited wellness offerings, but the natural environment provides a relaxing atmosphere.

No formal spa, but activities like guided walks are available.

Bars:

No on-site bar, but drinks are served during mealtimes.

Events and Conferences:

Perfect for small, exclusive corporate events or team-building activities in a unique setting.

Basic Facilities and Amenities:

- Free Wi-Fi in the main lodge
- Dining room serving locally-sourced food

- Outdoor pool
- Eco-friendly amenities like solar-powered lighting

Opening and Closing Hours:

Check-in: 3:00 PM

Check-out: 10:00 AM

Price:
Starting from AUD $800 per night (all-inclusive).

Pros:

- Immersive wildlife experience
- Eco-friendly accommodations in a pristine environment
- Secluded and peaceful location

Cons:

- Limited amenities and facilities
- Remote location may be difficult to access

Local Tips:

Join a morning or afternoon safari to spot local wildlife like crocodiles and wild buffalo.

Enjoy a traditional bush breakfast under the open sky.

3. Saffire Freycinet, Tasmania

Saffire Freycinet is a luxury eco-lodge situated in Tasmania's stunning Freycinet National Park. It blends modern architecture with sustainable practices, offering an unforgettable experience surrounded by nature.

Location:
Address: 2352 Coles Bay Road, Coles Bay, TAS 7215, Australia

Proximity: Located within Freycinet National Park, just a short drive from Coles Bay.

Highlights:

Spectacular views of the Hazards Mountains and Great Oyster Bay

Award-winning design focused on sustainability

Exclusive and tranquil environment

Spa and Wellness:

Saffire Spa offers a range of treatments, including organic facials and body therapies

Yoga and wellness retreats available

Bars:

The signature lounge offers a range of Tasmanian wines, craft beers, and cocktails.

Events and Conferences:

Ideal for small corporate retreats or events, with multiple function spaces available.

Basic Facilities and Amenities:

- Free Wi-Fi
- Pool and sauna
- Dining with a focus on Tasmanian produce
- Private balconies with each room

Opening and Closing Hours:

Check-in: 2:00 PM

Check-out: 11:00 AM

Price:
Starting from AUD $1,000 per night (including meals and some activities).

Pros:

- Stunning natural beauty and architectural design
- Exceptional focus on sustainability

- Great location for nature lovers

Cons:

- Pricey, especially during high season
- Limited access to nearby towns and attractions

Local Tips:

Hike to Wineglass Bay for breathtaking views.

Try the local oysters during your stay—they're some of the best in Australia.

4. The InterContinental Hayman Island Resort, Queensland

The InterContinental Hayman Island Resort is a luxury eco-conscious resort located in the heart of the Great Barrier Reef. It offers high-end service while maintaining a commitment to environmental sustainability.

Location:

Address: Hayman Island, Whitsundays, Queensland 4801, Australia

Proximity: Accessible via boat from Airlie Beach or helicopter from the mainland.

Highlights:

- Stunning beachfront location with exclusive access to the Great Barrier Reef
- Array of eco-tourism activities including snorkeling and diving
- Modern eco-luxury rooms with ocean views

Spa and Wellness:

Hayman Spa offers a range of organic treatments

Yoga and wellness programs

Bars:

Multiple bars with views of the Coral Sea, offering tropical cocktails and wines.

Events and Conferences:

Perfect for large conferences, weddings, or corporate events with various event spaces and support services.

Basic Facilities and Amenities:

- Free Wi-Fi
- Outdoor pool and fitness center
- Multiple dining options focusing on sustainable practices
- Luxurious rooms and suites

Opening and Closing Hours:

Check-in: 3:00 PM

Check-out: 12:00 PM

Price:
Starting from AUD $800 per night.

Pros:

- Located in a UNESCO World Heritage site
- Stunning beachfront with direct access to the reef
- Full-service luxury experience with eco-friendly initiatives

Cons:

- Remote, meaning higher travel costs
- High price point, especially in peak seasons

Local Tips:

Take a snorkeling or diving tour to the Great Barrier Reef.

Explore the surrounding islands via boat for a more relaxed experience.

5. Lake Crackenback Resort & Spa, New South Wales

Located in the Snowy Mountains, Lake Crackenback Resort & Spa offers luxury and eco-friendly accommodations perfect for both winter and summer activities. It focuses on sustainable tourism practices and provides a range of outdoor adventures.

Location:
Address: 1650 Alpine Way, Crackenback, NSW 2627, Australia

Proximity: Just 15 minutes from Thredbo and Perisher Ski Resorts, and a short drive from the Kosciuszko National Park.

Highlights:

Eco-friendly lodges and apartments with lake views

Year-round outdoor activities like skiing, hiking, and fishing

A focus on sustainable design and practices

Spa and Wellness:

Full-service spa offering rejuvenating treatments

Sauna and wellness packages available

Bars:

The resort has a cozy bar with views of the lake and mountains.

Events and Conferences:

Great for small corporate events and team-building retreats in a natural setting.

Basic Facilities and Amenities:

- Free Wi-Fi
- Full kitchen facilities in each room
- Outdoor pool and gym
- On-site restaurant with organic and locally sourced ingredients

Opening and Closing Hours:

Check-in: 3:00 PM

Check-out: 10:00 AM

Price:
Starting from AUD $300 per night.

Pros:

- Year-round activities for nature enthusiasts
- Excellent location for winter sports and hiking

- Focus on eco-tourism

Cons:

- Remote location may be difficult for some to access
- Limited luxury dining options nearby

Local Tips:

During winter, explore the nearby ski resorts of Perisher and Thredbo.

In warmer months, enjoy the numerous walking trails and wildlife watching.

Campgrounds and Glamping

Campgrounds and glamping in Australia provide unique opportunities for tourists to connect with nature. From traditional camping spots to luxurious glamping sites, these accommodations offer a range of experiences to suit all comfort levels. Perfect for exploring Australia's stunning landscapes, they combine adventure with relaxation, making them ideal for nature-loving travelers.

1. Wilsons Promontory National Park Campground, Victoria

Located in the stunning Wilsons Promontory National Park, this campground offers a rustic yet scenic experience surrounded by pristine beaches, lush forests, and abundant wildlife.

Location:

Address: Wilsons Promontory Road, Yanakie, VIC 3960, Australia

Proximity: 2.5 hours' drive from Melbourne.

Highlights:

- Stunning coastal and forest landscapes
- Access to hiking trails, including Mount Oberon and Squeaky Beach
- Abundant wildlife, including kangaroos and wombats

Spa and Wellness:

No formal spa, but nature walks and relaxation by the beach offer rejuvenation.

Bars:

No on-site bar; BYO for campfire evenings.

Events and Conferences:

No formal facilities, but great for group retreats or nature-based gatherings.

Basic Facilities and Amenities:

- Restrooms and hot showers
- Communal kitchen and barbecue areas
- Powered and unpowered campsites

Opening and Closing Hours:

Open year-round

Check-in: 2:00 PM

Check-out: 10:00 AM

Price:
Starting at AUD $40 per night per campsite.

Pros:

- Affordable and picturesque location
- Variety of activities, from hiking to beach lounging
- Family-friendly environment

Cons:

- Basic amenities, not suitable for luxury travelers
- Popular in peak seasons, so it gets crowded

Local Tips:

Book early, especially during school holidays.

Pack insect repellent to stay comfortable.

2. Longitude 131°, Northern Territory

Longitude 131° offers luxurious glamping in the heart of Australia, with breathtaking views of Uluru and the surrounding desert.

Location:
Address: Yulara Drive, Yulara, NT 0872, Australia

Proximity: 20 minutes from Ayers Rock Airport.

Highlights:

- Exclusive tented pavilions with direct views of Uluru
- Personalized tours of Uluru-Kata Tjuta National Park
- Sustainable luxury with minimal environmental impact

Spa and Wellness:

Dune House Spa offers treatments inspired by the outback's natural elements.

Bars:

On-site bar with a curated selection of Australian wines and spirits.

Events and Conferences:

Suitable for intimate gatherings or corporate retreats in a private setting.

Basic Facilities and Amenities:

- Free Wi-Fi
- Air-conditioned tents with luxury furnishings
- Gourmet dining included in the package

Opening and Closing Hours:

Check-in: 2:00 PM

Check-out: 10:30 AM

Price:
Starting at AUD $2,000 per night (all-inclusive).

Pros:

- Stunning and unique desert setting
- Exceptional service and exclusivity
- All-inclusive experience with gourmet meals

Cons:

- Expensive and remote
- Limited capacity; advance booking is essential

Local Tips:

Take advantage of stargazing sessions for an unforgettable experience.

Participate in sunrise or sunset tours of Uluru.

3. Paperbark Camp, New South Wales

Paperbark Camp offers eco-friendly glamping near the pristine beaches of Jervis Bay, combining luxury with nature.

Location:
Address: 571 Woollamia Road, Woollamia, NSW 2540, Australia

Proximity: 2.5 hours from Sydney.

Highlights:

- Safari-style tents nestled in bushland
- Close to Jervis Bay's white sandy beaches
- Canoeing and kayaking opportunities

Spa and Wellness:

In-room massages can be arranged.

Bars:

On-site bar with a selection of wines and craft beers.

Events and Conferences:

Ideal for weddings or small corporate retreats with nature-inspired themes.

Basic Facilities and Amenities:

- Free Wi-Fi in the main lodge
- Ensuite bathrooms with eco-friendly toiletries
- Complimentary bikes and canoes

Opening and Closing Hours:

Check-in: 2:00 PM

Check-out: 11:00 AM

Price:
Starting at AUD $500 per night.

Pros:

- Perfect blend of comfort and adventure
- Close proximity to beaches and water activities
- Strong focus on sustainability

Cons:

- May lack privacy due to the open nature of the tents
- Limited dining options in the vicinity

Local Tips:

Visit Jervis Bay for dolphin-watching cruises.

Try the signature bush tucker-inspired menu at the restaurant.

4. Bay of Fires Bush Retreat, Tasmania

A boutique glamping site near the iconic Bay of Fires, this retreat offers a tranquil escape with stylish, eco-friendly accommodations.

Location:
Address: 322 Ansons Bay Road, Binalong Bay, TAS 7216, Australia

Proximity: 10 minutes from the Bay of Fires.

Highlights:

- Close to the iconic Bay of Fires with its pristine beaches and vibrant orange rocks
- Unique glamping tents with wood-fired heating
- Communal campfire evenings

Spa and Wellness:

No spa services; the natural surroundings offer relaxation.

Bars:

BYO drinks are welcome at the communal areas.

Events and Conferences:

Great for small events like workshops or intimate celebrations.

Basic Facilities and Amenities:

- Shared kitchen and bathroom facilities
- Comfortable tents with plush bedding
- Outdoor dining areas

Opening and Closing Hours:

Check-in: 2:00 PM

Check-out: 10:00 AM

Price:
Starting at AUD $250 per night.

Pros:

- Affordable luxury in a stunning natural location
- Close to the Bay of Fires for outdoor activities
- Intimate and quiet atmosphere

Cons:

- Shared bathroom facilities may not suit everyone
- Limited amenities for longer stays

Local Tips:

Bring a good pair of walking shoes to explore the beaches and trails.

Visit during the off-season for more privacy.

5. Nightfall Camp, Queensland

Nestled in the rainforest near Lamington National Park, Nightfall Camp offers an exclusive and sustainable glamping experience.

Location:
Address: 3009 Christmas Creek Road, Lamington, QLD 4285, Australia
Proximity: 2 hours from Brisbane.

Highlights:

- Secluded luxury tents surrounded by rainforest

- Access to private swimming holes and hiking trails
- Gourmet meals cooked over an open fire

Spa and Wellness:

Natural hot springs nearby for a rejuvenating experience.

Bars:

No dedicated bar, but premium wines and craft beers are served during meals.

Events and Conferences:

Ideal for romantic getaways or small, private celebrations.

Basic Facilities and Amenities:

- Luxury tents with ensuite bathrooms
- Handcrafted furnishings and eco-friendly features
- Outdoor fire pits

Opening and Closing Hours:

Check-in: 3:00 PM

Check-out: 11:00 AM

Price:
Starting at AUD $1,200 per night (all-inclusive).

Pros:

- Exclusive and tranquil rainforest setting
- Exceptional food and personalized service
- Strong emphasis on sustainability

Cons:

- Expensive compared to other options
- Remote location with limited cell coverage

Local Tips:

Book a private tour of Lamington National Park for a unique experience.

Pack light but include weather-appropriate gear for rainforest conditions.

Chapter 4: Top Destinations
Sydney: Iconic Landmarks and Hidden Gems
Iconic Landmarks in Sydney

No visit to Sydney is complete without exploring its world-renowned landmarks, which showcase the city's rich history, culture, and stunning architecture.

Sydney Opera House:

A UNESCO World Heritage Site, this architectural marvel stands as a symbol of Australia. Take a guided tour to learn about its history, enjoy a world-class performance, or dine at one of its harborside restaurants.

Sydney Harbour Bridge:

Affectionately called "The Coathanger," this engineering masterpiece offers panoramic views of the city. For thrill-seekers, the **BridgeClimb** experience is a must, while others can enjoy a leisurely stroll across its pedestrian walkway.

Bondi Beach:

Famous for its golden sands and excellent surf, Bondi Beach is a hotspot for sunbathers and swimmers. Take the **Bondi to Coogee Coastal Walk** for spectacular views of the Pacific Ocean and Sydney's coastline.

The Rocks:

As Sydney's oldest neighborhood, The Rocks is a historic area with cobblestone streets, colonial-era buildings, boutique shops, and vibrant weekend markets.

Darling Harbour:

A bustling waterfront precinct featuring attractions such as the **SEA LIFE Sydney Aquarium**, **Wildlife Sydney Zoo**, and a variety of cafes, restaurants, and bars.

Hidden Gems in Sydney

Beyond the famous attractions, Sydney is brimming with lesser-known treasures waiting to be discovered.

Wendy's Secret Garden:

Located in Lavender Bay, this enchanting garden is a peaceful oasis filled with lush greenery, flowers, and views of the Sydney Harbour Bridge.

Paddington Reservoir Gardens:

A beautifully restored underground reservoir turned into a public garden, offering a tranquil spot away from the city's hustle and bustle.

Cockatoo Island:

A UNESCO World Heritage Site in Sydney Harbour, Cockatoo Island offers a fascinating history of shipbuilding and convict labor. You can camp overnight or explore its tunnels and industrial relics.

Barangaroo Reserve:

A stunning harborside park showcasing native Australian flora, Barangaroo Reserve is perfect for picnics, leisurely walks, or catching a ferry to other parts of the city.

Milk Beach:

A secluded spot in the affluent suburb of Vaucluse, Milk Beach offers breathtaking views of the city skyline and harbor.

Things to Do in Sydney

Cultural Experiences: Visit the **Art Gallery of New South Wales** or catch a performance at the **Capitol Theatre**.

Harbor Cruises: Explore Sydney's waterways on a harbor cruise, which offers unparalleled views of the city's landmarks.

Food and Drink: Savor Sydney's diverse culinary scene, from fresh seafood at **Sydney Fish Market** to trendy cafes in **Surry Hills**.

Outdoor Adventures: Hike through **Ku-ring-gai Chase National Park** or kayak along the Sydney Harbour.

Why Sydney is a Must-Visit Destination

Sydney's combination of world-class landmarks, vibrant culture, and hidden gems makes it a standout destination in Australia. Whether you're marveling at the Opera House, exploring its historic neighborhoods, or finding peace in a secret garden, Sydney offers something extraordinary for every traveler.

Melbourne: Culture, Art, and Food

Culture in Melbourne

Melbourne's culture is a rich tapestry influenced by its multicultural population and artistic heritage. The city is known for its festivals, live performances, and thriving creative scene.

Laneways and Street Art:

Melbourne's laneways, such as **Hosier Lane** and **AC/DC Lane**, are world-famous for their vibrant street art, making the city a living gallery.

Theatre and Live Music:

Home to iconic venues like the **Princess Theatre** and the **Forum Theatre**, Melbourne hosts numerous performances, from Broadway musicals to indie gigs.

Museums and Galleries:

National Gallery of Victoria (NGV): Australia's oldest and most prestigious art gallery, featuring an impressive collection of international and Australian art.

Melbourne Museum: Dive into Victoria's natural and cultural history, including exhibitions on the city's Indigenous heritage.

Festivals and Events:

Melbourne's calendar is packed with cultural festivals, including the **Melbourne International Comedy Festival**, **Melbourne Writers Festival**, and **Moomba Festival**, Australia's largest community event.

Art in Melbourne

The city's art scene is diverse and constantly evolving, with spaces that cater to both traditional and contemporary tastes.

Public Art Installations: Scattered throughout the city, installations like **Federation Square's architectural designs** and sculptures in public parks showcase Melbourne's commitment to art in everyday life.

Art Precincts:

Southbank: A cultural hub with theaters, galleries, and the iconic **Arts Centre Melbourne**.

Gertrude Street, Fitzroy: A hotspot for independent galleries and emerging artists.

Creative Workshops: Engage with local artists through workshops in pottery, painting, or photography, available in neighborhoods like **Collingwood** and **Brunswick**.

Food in Melbourne

Melbourne is a paradise for food lovers, boasting a culinary scene as diverse as its population. The city's obsession with quality ingredients and innovative dining ensures there's always something new to try.

Cafés and Coffee Culture: Renowned for its coffee, Melbourne takes its café culture seriously. Enjoy expertly brewed espresso at places like **Proud Mary** or **Axil Coffee Roasters**.

Fine Dining: World-class restaurants such as **Attica**, led by chef Ben Shewry, and **Vue de Monde**, offering stunning city views, redefine the dining experience.

Multicultural Cuisine:

Chinatown: Sample authentic Chinese, Japanese, and Thai cuisine.

Lygon Street: Melbourne's "Little Italy," famous for its pasta and gelato.

Footscray and Richmond: Known for incredible Vietnamese and African flavors.

Markets:

Queen Victoria Market: A bustling spot to savor international street food and shop for fresh produce.

South Melbourne Market: Perfect for trying local specialties like dim sims and oysters.

Why Visit Melbourne for Culture, Art, and Food?

Melbourne's seamless blend of cultural vibrancy, artistic innovation, and culinary excellence makes it a city like no other. Whether exploring its graffiti-filled laneways, attending a theatrical masterpiece, or indulging in its globally inspired cuisine, Melbourne captivates the senses and leaves lasting memories.

Brisbane and the Gold Coast: Beaches and Outdoor Adventures

Brisbane: A River City with Outdoor Appeal

Brisbane, known for its sunny weather and vibrant atmosphere, offers plenty of outdoor activities alongside its urban attractions.

South Bank Parklands:

This riverside gem features lush gardens, the **Streets Beach lagoon**, and cultural landmarks like the **Queensland Art Gallery** and **Gallery of Modern Art (QAGOMA)**.

The Brisbane River:

Take a **CityCat ferry** to explore the city or try kayaking along the river for a unique perspective of Brisbane's skyline.

Mount Coot-tha:

Just a short drive from the city, Mount Coot-tha offers breathtaking views and hiking trails. Don't miss the **Brisbane Botanic Gardens** at its base.

Lone Pine Koala Sanctuary:

Interact with native wildlife by cuddling a koala or hand-feeding kangaroos at this iconic sanctuary.

Gold Coast: Beach Paradise and Adventure Playground

The Gold Coast, just an hour south of Brisbane, is renowned for its golden sands, world-class surf, and adrenaline-pumping activities.

Beaches:

Surfers Paradise: The heart of the Gold Coast, perfect for surfing, sunbathing, and vibrant nightlife.

Burleigh Heads: A more relaxed atmosphere with excellent surf conditions and scenic walks.

Coolangatta: Known for its calm waters, ideal for families and beginner surfers.

Theme Parks:

The Gold Coast is home to Australia's best theme parks, including:

Dreamworld: Roller coasters and wildlife encounters.

Sea World: Marine life exhibits and water-themed rides.

Warner Bros. Movie World: Thrilling rides and cinematic experiences.

Hinterland Adventures:

Escape to the lush greenery of the Gold Coast Hinterland:

Lamington National Park: Explore rainforest trails, waterfalls, and the **Tree Top Walkway**.

Springbrook National Park: Marvel at the **Natural Bridge**, a stunning waterfall cascading through a cave.

Outdoor Adventures in Brisbane and the Gold Coast

Water Sports:

Try stand-up paddleboarding, jet-skiing, or snorkeling in the calm waters of **Moreton Bay** or the **Gold Coast Broadwater**.

Whale Watching:

From June to November, witness majestic humpback whales on their migration along the coast.

Skydiving:
Experience an adrenaline rush with tandem skydives offering incredible views of Brisbane or the Gold Coast.

Cycling and Walking Trails:

In Brisbane: The **Riverwalk** and paths through **New Farm Park** are scenic and accessible.

On the Gold Coast: The **Oceanway Path** hugs the coastline, perfect for casual walks or bike rides.

Why Brisbane and the Gold Coast are Must-Visit Destinations

Brisbane's warm hospitality and cultural vibe combined with the Gold Coast's idyllic beaches and adventurous spirit create the ultimate Queensland experience. Whether exploring bustling cityscapes, surfing legendary waves, or trekking through lush rainforests, this region promises memories that will last a lifetime.

Cairns and the Great Barrier Reef

The Great Barrier Reef: A World Wonder

The Great Barrier Reef, the world's largest coral reef system and a UNESCO World Heritage Site, stretches over 2,300 kilometers and teems with marine life.

Snorkeling and Scuba Diving:

Discover vibrant coral gardens, exotic fish, sea turtles, and more. Tours from Cairns take you to spectacular sites such as **Green Island**, **Fitzroy Island**, and the outer reef.

Glass-Bottom Boats and Semi-Submarines:

Perfect for non-swimmers, these tours offer an up-close view of the underwater marvels without getting wet.

Helicopter and Scenic Flights:

Experience the reef's breathtaking scale and beauty from above, with views of coral atolls, sand cays, and turquoise waters.

Overnight Cruises:

Stay on the reef for an unforgettable experience, watching the sunset and seeing marine life in its nocturnal splendor.

Cairns: A Tropical City with Adventure

Cairns is more than just a base for reef explorations. Its vibrant city center and nearby attractions make it a must-visit destination.

Cairns Esplanade Lagoon:

A popular waterfront spot with a free swimming lagoon, boardwalks, and picnic areas.

Night Markets:

Browse local crafts, souvenirs, and street food at the bustling **Cairns Night Markets.**

Kuranda Village:

Accessible by the **Kuranda Scenic Railway** or **Skyrail Rainforest Cableway**, this charming village features markets, wildlife parks, and cultural experiences.

Tjapukai Aboriginal Cultural Park:

Immerse yourself in Indigenous culture with performances, workshops, and storytelling by the Tjapukai people.

Daintree Rainforest and Cape Tribulation

Just north of Cairns lies the **Daintree Rainforest**, another UNESCO World Heritage Site and one of the oldest rainforests on Earth.

Daintree River Cruises:

Spot crocodiles, tropical birds, and other wildlife on a leisurely boat ride.

Mossman Gorge:

Walk through pristine rainforests and swim in crystal-clear freshwater pools.

Cape Tribulation:

Where the rainforest meets the reef, this remote area offers stunning beaches, jungle treks, and eco-adventures.

Outdoor Adventures in Cairns

Whitewater Rafting:

The **Barron River** and **Tully River** offer exhilarating rafting experiences for thrill-seekers.

Bungee Jumping and Ziplining:

Try an adrenaline-pumping bungee jump or zipline adventure in the lush rainforest with **AJ Hackett Cairns**.

Waterfalls Circuit:

Explore stunning waterfalls like **Millaa Millaa Falls**, **Josephine Falls**, and **Zillie Falls** in the nearby Atherton Tablelands.

Why Visit Cairns and the Great Barrier Reef?

Cairns and the Great Barrier Reef combine natural beauty, adventure, and cultural richness in one remarkable destination. Whether diving into the reef's wonders, trekking through ancient rainforests, or enjoying the city's tropical vibe, this region offers an unparalleled experience for every traveler.

Perth: Sunset Views and Coastal Life

Sunset Views in Perth

Perth is renowned for its spectacular sunsets, thanks to its location along the Indian Ocean.

Cottesloe Beach:

A local favorite, Cottesloe offers soft sands, turquoise waters, and unparalleled sunset views. Grab a spot on the beach or enjoy dinner at a waterfront café while the sun dips below the horizon.

Kings Park and Botanic Garden:

Overlooking the Swan River and Perth's skyline, this park is a serene spot for sunset picnics. The **DNA Tower** provides panoramic views, making it ideal for photographers.

Rottnest Island:

Just a ferry ride away, Rottnest Island is famous for its secluded beaches and incredible views. End the day at **Pinky Beach** or **Bathurst Lighthouse** for a tranquil sunset experience.

Coastal Life in Perth

Perth's coastline is dotted with pristine beaches and lively waterfronts, perfect for relaxation or adventure.

Scarborough Beach:

A buzzing hub for surfers, swimmers, and beachgoers, Scarborough offers a lively atmosphere with restaurants, markets, and events.

Fremantle:

This historic port city, just 30 minutes from Perth, blends maritime charm with modern vibes. Explore the **Fremantle Markets**, enjoy fresh seafood at the harbor, and stroll along **Bathers Beach**.

Hillarys Boat Harbour:

A family-friendly destination with sandy beaches, restaurants, and the **AQWA (Aquarium of Western Australia)**, showcasing local marine life.

Swan River:

The lifeblood of Perth, the Swan River offers scenic cruises, kayaking opportunities, and riverside trails for cycling or walking.

Outdoor Adventures in and Around Perth

Rottnest Island Adventures: Beyond its sunsets, the island offers snorkeling, cycling, and the chance to meet the adorable quokkas, often called "the happiest animals on Earth."

Pinnacles Desert: Located in Nambung National Park, a few hours north of Perth, this unique landscape features limestone formations that look otherworldly, especially at sunset.

Wave Rock: A natural granite formation shaped like a breaking wave, this iconic spot is a great day trip from Perth.

Penguin Island: A short ferry ride from Rockingham, this island is home to a colony of little penguins and is perfect for wildlife lovers.

Urban Attractions with a Coastal Vibe

Elizabeth Quay: This waterfront precinct blends modern architecture with recreational spaces. Take a walk along the arched suspension bridge or dine with a view of the city's skyline.

Perth Zoo: Located on the South Perth foreshore, the zoo showcases Australia's unique wildlife, including kangaroos and koalas.

Art and Culture: Visit the **Art Gallery of Western Australia** or explore Perth's street art scene for a creative fix.

Why Visit Perth?

Perth's charm lies in its ability to offer everything from serene beachside retreats to lively urban experiences. With its stunning sunsets, thriving coastal life, and access to natural wonders, Perth promises a refreshing escape for travelers seeking beauty and adventure.

Adelaide: Wine Regions and Festivals

Wine Regions Near Adelaide

Adelaide is the gateway to some of Australia's most renowned wine regions, offering exceptional wine-tasting experiences and picturesque landscapes.

Barossa Valley:

Located just an hour's drive from Adelaide, the Barossa Valley is famous for its rich Shiraz wines and charming cellar doors.

Visit iconic wineries such as **Penfolds** and **Jacob's Creek**.

Enjoy gourmet dining and farm-to-table experiences at **Maggie Beer's Farm Shop**.

Take a scenic hot air balloon ride over the vineyards for breathtaking views.

McLaren Vale:

This coastal wine region is known for its bold Grenache and sustainable viticulture.

Sample wines at **d'Arenberg Cube**, a quirky winery and art gallery.

Explore the **Shiraz Trail**, a cycling path that weaves through the vineyards.

Pair your wine with stunning ocean views at the **Star of Greece** restaurant.

Adelaide Hills:

Just 30 minutes from the city, this cool-climate region produces elegant Pinot Noir and Chardonnay.

Visit boutique wineries like **Bird in Hand** and **Shaw + Smith**.

Explore the quaint villages of **Hahndorf**, Australia's oldest German settlement, offering local produce and artisan goods.

Festivals in Adelaide

Adelaide is known as the "Festival City" for its packed calendar of world-class events and celebrations.

Adelaide Festival:

Held in March, this internationally acclaimed arts festival showcases theatre, music, dance, and visual arts from around the globe.

Adelaide Fringe:

Running alongside the Adelaide Festival, the Fringe is the largest open-access arts festival in the Southern Hemisphere, featuring comedy, cabaret, and street performances.

Tasting Australia:

A food and wine festival held in late autumn, offering exclusive dining events, cooking demonstrations, and regional food tours.

Barossa Vintage Festival:

A celebration of wine, food, and heritage in the Barossa Valley, featuring wine tastings, grape stomping, and cultural events.

Santos Tour Down Under:

Australia's premier cycling race, held in January, brings an exciting mix of sport and entertainment to the city.

Other Attractions in and Around Adelaide

Glenelg Beach:

A short tram ride from the city, Glenelg offers pristine beaches, bustling cafés, and a relaxed seaside vibe.

Adelaide Central Market:

A food lover's paradise, this iconic market offers fresh produce, artisan goods, and multicultural cuisine.

Cleland Wildlife Park:

Get up close with koalas, kangaroos, and other native wildlife in this family-friendly park located in the Adelaide Hills.

North Terrace:

Stroll along this cultural boulevard, home to the **Art Gallery of South Australia**, the **South Australian Museum**, and the **Adelaide Botanic Garden**.

Why Visit Adelaide?

Adelaide's charm lies in its seamless blend of world-class wine, lively festivals, and relaxed city life. Whether you're sipping premium vintages in the Barossa Valley, soaking in the energy of a global festival, or savoring local produce at a bustling market, Adelaide promises a rich and memorable experience for every traveler.

Hobart and Tasmania: Wilderness and Heritage
Historic Heritage of Hobart

Salamanca Place and Battery Point:

Stroll through Salamanca Place, a row of 19th-century sandstone warehouses now home to art galleries, boutiques, and cafes. Nearby, Battery Point features charming colonial cottages and cobblestone streets that reflect Hobart's maritime past.

Tasmanian Museum and Art Gallery (TMAG):

Discover Tasmania's natural history, Indigenous heritage, and colonial legacy at this comprehensive museum located in Hobart's historic waterfront precinct.

Port Arthur Historic Site:

A short drive from Hobart, this UNESCO World Heritage-listed site is one of Australia's most significant convict-era locations. Take a guided tour to explore its haunting ruins and compelling history.

Richmond Village:

This picturesque village features Australia's oldest bridge still in use, built by convicts in 1823. It's also home to charming heritage buildings and cozy tearooms.

Tasmania's Wilderness Adventures

Tasmania is famous for its pristine wilderness areas, many of which are part of the Tasmanian Wilderness World Heritage Area.

Mount Wellington (kunanyi):

Towering over Hobart, Mount Wellington offers panoramic views of the city, harbor, and surrounding wilderness. Explore hiking trails, cycling paths, or simply drive to the summit for breathtaking vistas.

Freycinet National Park and Wineglass Bay:

A few hours' drive from Hobart, this national park is home to one of the world's most beautiful beaches, Wineglass Bay. Enjoy hiking, kayaking, and wildlife spotting in this coastal paradise.

Cradle Mountain-Lake St Clair National Park:

Famous for the Overland Track, this park offers alpine landscapes, ancient rainforests, and encounters with Tasmanian wildlife such as wombats and echidnas.

Bruny Island:

A short ferry ride from Hobart, Bruny Island combines dramatic cliffs, pristine beaches, and gourmet delights like artisan cheeses, oysters, and wines. Don't miss the breathtaking views from the Neck Lookout.

Wildlife and Unique Experiences

Bonorong Wildlife Sanctuary:

Located near Hobart, this sanctuary lets you encounter iconic Tasmanian devils, kangaroos, and wombats up close while supporting conservation efforts.

Maria Island:

Known for its well-preserved convict history and abundant wildlife, including wombats and Cape Barren geese, Maria Island is a haven for nature and history enthusiasts.

Hobart's Cultural and Culinary Scene

Salamanca Market:

Held every Saturday, this vibrant market offers local crafts, fresh produce, and street performances, making it a favorite for visitors and locals alike.

MONA (Museum of Old and New Art):

A world-renowned museum featuring provocative and contemporary art exhibits. The ferry ride to MONA, with its stylish design and views of the Derwent River, is an experience in itself.

Local Food and Drink:

Hobart is known for its fresh seafood, cool-climate wines, and craft spirits. Don't miss the chance to sample locally sourced oysters, salmon, and whisky at spots like the **Lark Distillery** and **Mures Upper Deck**.

Why Visit Hobart and Tasmania?

Hobart and Tasmania are a treasure trove of wilderness, heritage, and charm. Whether you're exploring historic convict sites, hiking in World Heritage-listed landscapes, or indulging in local culinary delights, Tasmania offers an unforgettable journey into Australia's natural and cultural riches.

Darwin: Outback Adventures and Indigenous Culture

Outback Adventures Near Darwin

Kakadu National Park:

A UNESCO World Heritage Site, Kakadu is a short drive from Darwin and showcases diverse ecosystems, ancient rock art, and breathtaking landscapes.

Explore towering waterfalls like **Jim Jim Falls** and **Twin Falls**.

Discover Aboriginal rock art galleries at **Ubirr** and **Nourlangie**.

Spot saltwater crocodiles and bird species on a **Yellow Water Billabong cruise**.

Litchfield National Park:

Known for its dramatic waterfalls, crystal-clear swimming holes, and termite mounds, Litchfield is an ideal day trip from Darwin. Swim at **Florence Falls** or enjoy the serene beauty of **Buley Rockhole**.

Nitmiluk National Park (Katherine Gorge):

Take a scenic cruise, kayak through the stunning gorges, or hike the trails to experience the rugged beauty of this park located south of Darwin.

Indigenous Culture and Heritage

Darwin is a rich cultural hub, offering insight into Australia's Indigenous heritage and traditions.

Tiwi Islands:

A short flight or ferry from Darwin, the Tiwi Islands are home to the Tiwi people, known for their vibrant art and unique traditions. Join a cultural tour to learn about their way of life and enjoy local performances.

Darwin Aboriginal Art Fair:

Held annually in August, this event celebrates Indigenous art from across Australia, featuring exhibitions, workshops, and opportunities to purchase authentic works.

Pudakul Aboriginal Cultural Tours:

Located just outside Darwin, these tours offer hands-on experiences like didgeridoo playing, basket weaving, and bush tucker tasting.

Museum and Art Gallery of the Northern Territory (MAGNT):

Explore exhibits on Aboriginal art, history, and the region's natural environment, including the Cyclone Tracy display.

Other Highlights in Darwin

Mindil Beach Sunset Market:

Held during the dry season, this iconic market offers international cuisine, handmade crafts, and live entertainment against a backdrop of spectacular sunsets.

Darwin Waterfront Precinct:

Relax in the wave pool, swim in the safe lagoon, or dine at waterfront restaurants offering fresh seafood and tropical flavors.

Crocodylus Park and Crocosaurus Cove:

Get up close with saltwater crocodiles and learn about their habitats. For the daring, the "Cage of Death" experience at Crocosaurus Cove allows you to swim alongside these fascinating reptiles.

Darwin Military Museum: Discover Darwin's role in World War II through interactive exhibits and historic artifacts.

Tropical Adventures and Coastal Life

Darwin's tropical climate makes it ideal for outdoor activities year-round.

Fishing Charters:

Try your hand at catching barramundi, a prized local fish, in Darwin's pristine waters.

Cycling Trails:

Explore Darwin's scenic coastline and parks on the city's well-maintained cycling paths.

Sunset Cruises:

Sail along the harbor on a luxury catamaran or traditional pearling lugger while enjoying stunning sunsets over the Timor Sea.

Why Visit Darwin?

Darwin offers an unparalleled mix of outdoor adventures, rich Indigenous culture, and tropical relaxation. Whether you're exploring the ancient wonders of Kakadu, enjoying fresh seafood by the waterfront, or immersing yourself in Aboriginal traditions, Darwin promises a unique and unforgettable experience in Australia's rugged north.

Chapter 5: Must-See Attractions
Sydney Opera House and Harbour Bridge

The Sydney Opera House is one of the most iconic structures in the world, known for its unique sail-like design. The Sydney Harbour Bridge, often referred to as the "Coathanger," offers a stunning view of the city and harbor.

History

Sydney Opera House: Opened in 1973, it was designed by Danish architect Jørn Utzon and has become a symbol of Australia. It hosts world-class performances in music, dance, and theatre.

Sydney Harbour Bridge: Completed in 1932, the bridge is an engineering marvel and links Sydney's central business district with the North Shore.

Location

The Opera House is located at Bennelong Point, Circular Quay, Sydney.

The Harbour Bridge is located near The Rocks, just a short walk from the Opera House.

Opening Hours

Sydney Opera House: Open daily from 9:00 AM to 5:00 PM, but performances vary. Check the schedule for specific events.

Sydney Harbour Bridge: Open year-round for walking and cycling, with the BridgeClimb tours available from 7:00 AM to 6:00 PM.

Top Things to Do

Sydney Opera House: Attend a live performance, take a guided tour, or simply admire the architecture.

Sydney Harbour Bridge: Take a BridgeClimb for breathtaking views, walk or cycle across the bridge, or enjoy a scenic harbor cruise.

Practical Information

Tickets for the Opera House performances must be booked in advance.

The BridgeClimb requires a booking and has a minimum age requirement of 8 years.

Tips for Visiting

Arrive early to avoid crowds, especially for performances at the Opera House.

Wear comfortable shoes for walking or climbing the Harbour Bridge.

Consider a combined Opera House and BridgeClimb package for a unique experience.

Uluru (Ayers Rock)

Uluru is a massive sandstone monolith located in the heart of the Northern Territory. It's known for its stunning red color, especially at sunrise and sunset, and holds deep cultural significance for the local Anangu people.

History

Uluru has been a sacred site for the Anangu people for over 60,000 years. It was named Ayers Rock in 1873 after Sir Henry Ayers, but was returned to its traditional name, Uluru, in 1985.

Location

Uluru is situated in the Uluru-Kata Tjuta National Park, about 450 kilometers southwest of Alice Springs.

Opening Hours

The park is open year-round, from sunrise to sunset, but specific tours and activities have their own schedules.

Top Things to Do

Watch the sunrise and sunset, where the rock changes color dramatically.

Take a guided tour to learn about the Anangu culture.

Explore the nearby Kata Tjuta rock formations.

Walk around the base of Uluru or take a scenic helicopter flight.

Practical Information

The entrance fee for the park is valid for three days, so it's worth staying multiple days to explore fully.

It's important to respect the cultural significance of Uluru and refrain from climbing it.

Tips for Visiting

The weather can be extreme, so dress appropriately for both the heat and cold.

Carry plenty of water and sunscreen.

Be mindful of the Anangu people's wishes to not climb Uluru.

The Great Barrier Reef

The Great Barrier Reef is the world's largest coral reef system, stretching over 2,300 kilometers along the Queensland coast. It's home to a rich variety of marine life and one of the most popular diving and snorkeling destinations in the world.

History

The reef was designated a UNESCO World Heritage site in 1981 and is considered one of the seven natural wonders of the world. It's been formed over millions of years.

Location

The Great Barrier Reef is located off the coast of Queensland, with popular access points from Cairns, Port Douglas, and Airlie Beach.

Opening Hours

The reef is accessible year-round, with tours operating daily. Some resorts and attractions may have varying hours.

Top Things to Do

Snorkel or dive to explore the vibrant coral gardens and marine life.

Take a scenic flight over the reef for a bird's-eye view.

Visit the reef's islands, like Green Island or Fitzroy Island.

Participate in eco-friendly reef tours and educational programs.

Practical Information

The reef is best explored via guided tours, which often include transportation, equipment, and marine biologists to guide the experience.

The water can be chilly even in warm weather, so bring a wetsuit if you're sensitive to cold.

Tips for Visiting

Use reef-safe sunscreen to protect both your skin and the reef.

If you're a beginner diver, consider a guided diving tour.

Stay hydrated and wear light clothing to manage the tropical heat.

Great Ocean Road

The Great Ocean Road is one of the most scenic coastal drives in the world, stretching 243 kilometers from Torquay to Allansford in Victoria. It offers breathtaking views of cliffs, beaches, and the Southern Ocean.

History

The road was built between 1919 and 1932 as a memorial to soldiers who fought in World War I. It was originally intended to connect isolated coastal communities.

Location

The Great Ocean Road begins in Torquay, about 100 kilometers from Melbourne, and ends in Allansford.

Opening Hours

The road is open year-round, and it's best explored at your own pace, though some attractions like the Twelve Apostles may have specific opening hours.

Top Things to Do

Visit the Twelve Apostles, a series of limestone formations rising out of the sea.

Stop at Loch Ard Gorge, a site with historical significance and beautiful natural scenery.

Explore the Otway National Park and its waterfalls.

Go wildlife spotting for koalas and kangaroos.

Practical Information

The Great Ocean Road is best enjoyed over multiple days, as there are numerous stops and scenic lookouts.

Renting a car or taking a guided tour is the best way to explore the road.

Tips for Visiting

Be prepared for windy conditions, especially along the cliffside areas.

Pack snacks, as some areas are quite remote with few services.

Don't rush; the road is all about taking in the scenery and enjoying the journey.

Kakadu National Park

Kakadu National Park is a vast and diverse UNESCO World Heritage-listed site, located in the Northern Territory. It offers a unique blend of stunning landscapes, ancient Aboriginal rock art, and rich wildlife.

History

Kakadu has been inhabited by Indigenous people for over 65,000 years. The park's cultural and natural significance led to its designation as a World Heritage site in 1981.

Location

Kakadu National Park is located approximately 171 kilometers southeast of Darwin, the capital of the Northern Territory.

Opening Hours

The park is open year-round, though some specific areas may be closed during the wet season (November to April). Visitor centers are open daily from 8:00 AM to 5:00 PM.

Top Things to Do

Explore the ancient rock art at Ubirr and Nourlangie.

Take a boat cruise on Yellow Water Billabong to spot crocodiles and birdlife.

Hike to the top of Gunlom Falls or visit Jim Jim Falls.

Visit the Bowali Visitor Centre for information on the park's history and wildlife.

Practical Information

The park entry fee is applicable, and permits are required for certain activities.

Kakadu is vast, so it's best to plan several days for exploration.

Tips for Visiting

Carry insect repellent and sunscreen to protect yourself from the harsh tropical environment.

Respect local Indigenous cultures by avoiding restricted areas and following park guidelines.

The Twelve Apostles

The Twelve Apostles are a collection of limestone stacks located off the coast of the Great Ocean Road in Victoria. These natural formations are one of Australia's most iconic coastal landmarks.

History

The Twelve Apostles were formed over millions of years by erosion of the mainland coastline. While there were originally twelve, only eight remain due to natural erosion.

Location

The Twelve Apostles are located along the Great Ocean Road, near Port Campbell in Victoria, Australia.

Opening Hours

The site is accessible year-round, and the viewing platform is open from sunrise to sunset.

Top Things to Do

Take in panoramic views of the Twelve Apostles from the lookout platform.

Explore the nearby Loch Ard Gorge and Gibson Steps for more dramatic coastal views.

Enjoy scenic helicopter tours for a unique aerial perspective.

Practical Information

There are parking areas and picnic facilities near the Twelve Apostles.

The site is wheelchair accessible, with viewing platforms designed for optimal viewing.

Tips for Visiting

Visit early in the morning or late in the afternoon for the best lighting and fewer crowds.

Be mindful of the weather conditions, as coastal winds can be strong.

Fraser Island

Fraser Island, the world's largest sand island, is a UNESCO World Heritage site located off the coast of Queensland. Known for its diverse ecosystems, including rainforests, freshwater lakes, and sand dunes, it's a popular destination for nature lovers.

History

Fraser Island has a rich Indigenous history, with the Butchulla people being the traditional owners of the island. The island was first explored by Europeans in the 19th century.

Location

Fraser Island is located off the coast of Hervey Bay in Queensland, accessible by ferry.

Opening Hours

The island is open year-round, though access to some areas may be restricted during the wet season (November to April).

Top Things to Do

Drive along 75 Mile Beach, a designated highway for 4WD vehicles.

Swim in the crystal-clear waters of Lake McKenzie.

Hike through the rainforests of Central Station.

Spot wildlife like dingoes and colorful bird species.

Practical Information

4WD vehicles are necessary for travel around the island, and some tours offer guided experiences.

Camping permits are required for overnight stays in designated areas.

Tips for Visiting

Be cautious of the dingoes on the island, and never feed them.

Bring plenty of water and supplies, as services on the island are limited.

The Whitsundays

The Whitsunday Islands are a group of 74 islands located in the heart of the Great Barrier Reef. Known for their crystal-clear waters, white sandy beaches, and vibrant marine life, the Whitsundays are a tropical paradise.

History

The islands were named by Captain James Cook in 1770, as he passed through the area on Whit Sunday (a Christian holiday). They have since become a popular tourist destination.

Location

The Whitsundays are located off the coast of Queensland, with access points from Airlie Beach and Hamilton Island.

Opening Hours

The islands are accessible year-round, with various activities available depending on the season. Most tours operate from 7:00 AM to 5:00 PM.

Top Things to Do

Snorkel or dive at the Great Barrier Reef.

Relax on the pristine sands of Whitehaven Beach.

Take a scenic flight over the islands for an aerial view.

Sail through the islands or take a boat tour to explore secluded beaches.

Practical Information

Accommodation options range from luxury resorts to budget-friendly hostels.

It's important to book tours in advance, as the area is very popular during peak seasons.

Tips for Visiting

Bring reef-safe sunscreen and a hat to protect yourself from the tropical sun.

Keep an eye on weather conditions, as the region can experience storms in the wet season.

National Parks and Wildlife Sanctuaries

Australia boasts a wide variety of national parks and wildlife sanctuaries that protect its unique flora and fauna. These parks offer incredible opportunities for outdoor activities and wildlife viewing.

History

National parks and wildlife sanctuaries in Australia were established to protect its diverse ecosystems, which include tropical rainforests, deserts, and coastal environments. Many parks are also of cultural significance to Indigenous peoples.

Location

National parks are spread across Australia, with popular locations in every state. Notable parks include Kakadu National Park, Daintree Rainforest, and Wilsons Promontory.

Opening Hours

Most parks are open year-round, but specific attractions or trails may be closed during the wet season or for maintenance.

Top Things to Do

Hike through rainforests, mountains, or deserts.

Spot native wildlife, such as kangaroos, koalas, and rare bird species.

Participate in eco-tours and educational programs that highlight conservation efforts.

Enjoy water activities like canoeing, snorkeling, and fishing in designated areas.

Practical Information

Entry fees may apply for some parks, and camping permits are often required.

Guided tours and ranger programs are often available for an enhanced experience.

Tips for Visiting

Always carry enough water, especially when hiking in remote areas.

Respect park rules, including not disturbing wildlife and staying on designated paths.

Wear sturdy shoes and sun protection, as conditions can be harsh in many areas.

Chapter 6: Outdoor Activities
Hiking and Bushwalking

Popular Hiking and Bushwalking Trails

The Overland Track (Tasmania): This 6-day, 65km trek through Tasmania's wilderness is one of Australia's most iconic hikes. It passes through alpine meadows, ancient forests, and rugged mountains, offering stunning views and a chance to disconnect from the world.

Larapinta Trail (Northern Territory): Spanning 223km, the Larapinta Trail is a challenging, multi-day trek through the West MacDonnell Ranges. Known for its desert landscapes and Aboriginal cultural significance, it typically takes 14 days to complete.

Blue Mountains (New South Wales): Famous for its dramatic cliffs, valleys, and the **Three Sisters** rock formation, the Blue Mountains offer hikes like the **Grand Canyon Walk**, as well as the more challenging **Six Foot Track**, a 3-day trek across stunning scenery.

Kakadu National Park (Northern Territory): Kakadu is renowned for its biodiversity and Aboriginal culture. Trails like the **Nourlangie Rock Walk** and **Ubirr Walk** take you past ancient rock art and provide incredible views of wetlands and floodplains.

Wilson's Promontory (Victoria): Located at the southern tip of mainland Australia, Wilson's Promontory offers coastal walks through forests and beaches. The **Prom Walk** is a popular 2-3 day hike that showcases the park's diverse landscapes and wildlife.

Grampians National Park (Victoria): The Grampians are known for their rugged mountains and spectacular waterfalls. The **Mount William Summit** and **MacKenzie Falls Walk** offer stunning vistas of the region's natural beauty.

Daintree Rainforest (Queensland): The Daintree is one of the oldest rainforests in the world, with trails like the **Mossman Gorge Walk** leading you through lush, tropical landscapes filled with unique wildlife and plant species.

Wilpena Pound (South Australia): A natural amphitheater in the **Flinders Ranges**, Wilpena Pound offers some of the best hiking in the region, with the **St Mary's Peak** hike providing panoramic views of the surrounding landscape.

Types of Hikes

Short Walks: Perfect for those with limited time or casual walkers, these hikes are typically under 5km. Popular examples include the **Kings Canyon Rim Walk** and short coastal walks in national parks like **Grampians** and **Kakadu**.

Moderate Hikes: These hikes range from 5-15km and offer a bit more challenge, with hikes like the **Cedar Creek Falls Walk** in Queensland and the **Grand Canyon Walk** in the Blue Mountains. They usually take 3-6 hours to complete.

Long Hikes: For seasoned trekkers, long-distance hikes like the **Overland Track** and **Larapinta Trail** offer multi-day journeys through some of Australia's most remote and rugged landscapes.

Bushwalking Tips and Safety

Prepare for the Weather: Australia's weather can be unpredictable. Ensure you are prepared for the hot sun, rain, or colder temperatures by wearing layers and using sunscreen.

Hydration: It's crucial to carry enough water, especially in hot or dry regions, where dehydration is a real risk.

Know Your Route: Before embarking on a hike, make sure to research your trail, check weather conditions, and ensure your chosen path is safe.

Wildlife: Be aware of the potential presence of snakes, spiders, and other wildlife, particularly in remote areas. Always follow safety guidelines for wildlife encounters.

Navigation: Many bushwalking trails, especially in more remote areas, may not be well signposted. Carry a map or GPS device and familiarize yourself with basic navigation skills.

Pack Light: Keep your gear to a minimum while ensuring you have the essentials: water, snacks, first aid kit, and appropriate clothing.

Inform Someone: Always tell someone your hiking plans, particularly if you are heading into remote areas.

Surfing and Beach Activities

Top Surfing Destinations

Byron Bay (New South Wales): Known for its laid-back vibe, Byron Bay offers great surf spots for all levels, from **The Pass** (perfect for beginners) to **Wategos Beach** (popular with experienced surfers).

Gold Coast (Queensland): Famous for its consistent waves and surf culture, the Gold Coast features iconic spots like **Snapper Rocks** and **Kirra Beach**, attracting both pro surfers and beginners.

Bondi Beach (New South Wales): One of Australia's most famous beaches, Bondi is perfect for surf lessons with easy waves and plenty of surf schools to choose from.

Margaret River (Western Australia): This renowned surfing destination offers powerful waves for advanced surfers at **North Point** and **The Box**, while beginners can enjoy the relaxed atmosphere at **Prevelly Beach**.

Bells Beach (Victoria): Home to the annual Rip Curl Pro, Bells Beach is a must-visit for experienced surfers seeking big, challenging waves.

Coffs Harbour (New South Wales): With a variety of surf spots, including **Park Beach** and **Shelly Beach**, Coffs Harbour offers great options for surfers of all levels.

Other Beach Activities

Snorkeling and Scuba Diving: Many of Australia's beaches are gateways to vibrant coral reefs and marine life. Popular spots include the **Great Barrier Reef**, **Ningaloo Reef** (Western Australia), and **Wilson's Promontory** (Victoria).

Stand-Up Paddleboarding (SUP): Paddleboarding has gained popularity along Australia's calm beaches. Try it in places like **Noosa Heads (Queensland)** or **Palm Cove (Queensland)** for a relaxing and scenic experience.

Swimming and Sunbathing: Australia's beaches offer plenty of opportunities to relax and enjoy the sun. Iconic spots like **Bondi, Manly Beach**, and **Whitehaven Beach (Queensland)** provide clear waters and golden sands, perfect for a day of lounging.

Beach Volleyball: Many beaches, like **Bondi** and **Noosa**, have volleyball courts where you can join in on a friendly game.

Kayaking and Canoeing: Paddle along Australia's beautiful beaches and coastal areas. Try **Lake Macquarie (New South Wales)** or **Bells Beach** for tranquil water adventures.

Beach Safety Tips

Swim Between the Flags: Always swim at patrolled beaches between the red and yellow flags to ensure you're in a safe area.

Know the Conditions: Be aware of tides, rips, and currents before heading into the water. Check local surf reports or talk to lifeguards for the best conditions.

Wear Sun Protection: The Australian sun can be intense. Apply sunscreen, wear a hat, and cover up with protective clothing when not in the water.

Respect the Environment: Be mindful of wildlife and coral reefs, and avoid touching or disturbing marine life.

Stay Hydrated: The beach can be hot, so drink plenty of water, especially after swimming or surfing.

Scuba Diving and Snorkeling

Scuba Diving Destinations

Great Barrier Reef (Queensland): The world's largest coral reef system, the Great Barrier Reef is home to an incredible array of marine life. Popular dive sites include **Osprey Reef, Ribbon Reef No. 9**, and **Agincourt Reef**, offering diverse underwater scenery and encounters with sea turtles, sharks, and vibrant coral.

Ningaloo Reef (Western Australia): A UNESCO World Heritage Site, Ningaloo Reef is known for its clear waters and abundant marine life, including whale sharks, manta rays, and colorful fish. **Exmouth** and **Coral Bay** are excellent base camps for diving and snorkeling here.

Fraser Island (Queensland): Dive sites off the coast of Fraser Island offer shipwrecks, coral reefs, and diverse marine life, including reef sharks and dolphins. **Cathedrals** and **Pinnacles** are popular dive spots.

Heron Island (Queensland): Located within the Great Barrier Reef Marine Park, Heron Island offers excellent snorkeling and diving opportunities, with encounters with sea turtles, reef sharks, and a variety of fish species.

Port Douglas (Queensland): A gateway to the Great Barrier Reef, Port Douglas offers easy access to stunning dive sites like **Agincourt Reef** and **Opal Reef**, where you can see a range of reef fish and colorful coral formations.

Turtle Reef (Northern Queensland): A favorite for night diving, Turtle Reef allows divers to explore the reef after dark, witnessing creatures like giant clams, seahorses, and moray eels.

Snorkeling Spots

Great Barrier Reef (Queensland): Snorkelers can access shallow reef areas to see colorful fish, coral, and other marine life. Popular spots include **Green Island, Cairns Outer Reef**, and **Lady Elliot Island**.

Ningaloo Reef (Western Australia): Snorkelers can swim alongside whale sharks and manta rays in calm, clear waters. **Coral Bay** and **Exmouth** are ideal launch points for snorkeling tours.

Whitsundays (Queensland): The crystal-clear waters of the Whitsunday Islands offer fantastic snorkeling opportunities around **Heart Reef, Langford Reef**, and **Blue Pearl Bay**, where you can see colorful fish and stunning coral formations.

Lord Howe Island (New South Wales): Known for its clear waters and diverse marine life, snorkeling here allows visitors to explore vibrant coral gardens and see species like clownfish and sea turtles.

Fraser Island (Queensland): Snorkelers can access the island's coastal lagoons and shallow waters, where they'll find plenty of colorful fish and coral.

South Stradbroke Island (Queensland): A quieter alternative to the more popular beaches, South Stradbroke Island features calm waters and great snorkeling spots where you can see a variety of fish and sea life.

Marine Life and Coral Reefs

Whale Sharks: Ningaloo Reef is known for its encounters with gentle whale sharks during the annual whale shark season from March to July.

Manta Rays: Dive sites like **Lady Elliot Island** and **Heron Island** offer opportunities to see these graceful creatures.

Turtles: Snorkelers and divers can see various species of sea turtles, including green and loggerhead turtles, throughout the Great Barrier Reef and Ningaloo Reef.

Tropical Fish: Encounter a wide variety of colorful reef fish, such as parrotfish, clownfish, and angel fish, across Australia's reefs.

Coral Gardens: The Great Barrier Reef, Ningaloo Reef, and other dive sites feature stunning coral formations, from soft corals to brain and staghorn varieties.

Scuba Diving and Snorkeling Tips

Safety First: Always ensure you have a basic understanding of snorkeling or diving safety. If needed, take a course or hire a guide.

Gear: Wear a wetsuit if the water is cold, and use proper snorkeling or diving gear (mask, fins, snorkel) for comfort and visibility.

Marine Conservation: Respect the underwater environment and avoid touching or disturbing the marine life or coral.

Protect Your Skin: Use reef-safe sunscreen to protect delicate reef ecosystems.

Guided Tours: Consider booking a guided snorkeling or diving tour, especially if you're new to the activity, as local experts can lead you to the best spots and ensure safety.

Location and Timing: Certain areas, like the Great Barrier Reef and Ningaloo Reef, are best visited during the dry season (April to October) when the weather is clearer and calmer.

Snorkeling with Whale Sharks
Top Destination: Ningaloo Reef, Western Australia

The best place in Australia—and one of the best in the world—to snorkel with whale sharks is **Ningaloo Reef**, a UNESCO World Heritage Site. Located along the Coral Coast of Western Australia, this pristine reef system hosts annual whale shark migrations between **March and July**, offering snorkelers a chance to see these magnificent creatures up close.

Why Ningaloo Reef?

Ningaloo Reef's clear, calm waters provide excellent visibility, making it easier to spot and snorkel with whale sharks. Unlike many locations where diving is required, Ningaloo's shallow waters allow you to experience these majestic creatures with just a snorkel and mask.

What to Expect

Tours typically begin with a boat ride out to the reef, guided by experienced marine biologists and snorkel instructors. Spotter planes are often used to locate the whale sharks, ensuring the best chances of an encounter. Once a whale shark is sighted, small groups of snorkelers enter the water to observe and swim alongside these gentle giants while maintaining a respectful distance.

The Whale Shark Experience

Swimming alongside a whale shark is both humbling and exhilarating. These creatures can grow up to 12 meters (40 feet) in length but move with a calm, unhurried grace. While snorkeling, you might see their spotted patterns glimmering in the sunlight as they feed on plankton near the surface.

Best Time to Visit

The whale shark season at Ningaloo Reef runs from **March to July**, with April and May being peak months. During this time, the reef's waters are warm, and plankton blooms attract whale sharks to the area.

Other Activities at Ningaloo Reef

While snorkeling with whale sharks is the highlight, Ningaloo Reef offers plenty of additional marine adventures:

Snorkeling with **manta rays** and turtles.

Exploring vibrant coral gardens and tropical fish.

Seasonal encounters with **humpback whales** from June to November.

Tips for Snorkeling with Whale Sharks

Book with Reputable Operators: Choose eco-certified tours that prioritize the safety and well-being of the whale sharks.

Practice Snorkeling Skills: Ensure you're comfortable using a mask and snorkel before heading out.

Follow Guidelines: Keep a minimum distance of 3 meters (10 feet) from the whale shark's body and 4 meters (13 feet) from its tail. Avoid touching or blocking its path.

Stay Calm: Move slowly and avoid sudden movements to ensure a stress-free encounter for both you and the whale shark.

Use Reef-Safe Sunscreen: Protect both your skin and the environment with biodegradable sunscreen.

Bring an Underwater Camera: Capture the incredible moments, but don't forget to soak in the experience without distractions.

Camping and Wilderness Adventures

Top Camping Destinations

Uluru-Kata Tjuta National Park (Northern Territory)

Camp under the stars near the iconic Uluru, one of Australia's most sacred and awe-inspiring landmarks. The nearby **Ayers Rock Campground** provides basic amenities while keeping you close to the natural beauty of the desert.

Daintree Rainforest (Queensland)

One of the world's oldest rainforests, the Daintree offers unique camping experiences surrounded by lush greenery, exotic wildlife, and ancient ecosystems. The **Cape Tribulation Camping** site offers beachfront camping with eco-friendly facilities.

Flinders Ranges (South Australia)

Explore the rugged beauty of Australia's oldest mountain range with campgrounds like **Wilpena Pound**, offering access to hiking trails, wildlife spotting, and breathtaking views of red-hued landscapes.

Freycinet National Park (Tasmania)

Famous for its white sand beaches and turquoise waters, Freycinet is a haven for campers. **Wineglass Bay** and **Honeymoon Bay** campsites provide stunning views and proximity to hiking trails.

Great Otway National Park (Victoria)

Located along the Great Ocean Road, this park features coastal cliffs, waterfalls, and lush forests. **Johanna Beach Campground** is a favorite for its ocean views and relaxed vibe.

Wilderness Activities

Bushwalking and Hiking: Many camping locations feature well-marked trails for exploring the surrounding landscapes. Popular options include the **Larapinta Trail** in the Northern Territory and the **Overland Track** in Tasmania.

Wildlife Spotting: Keep an eye out for kangaroos, koalas, wombats, and rare bird species in their natural habitats.

Stargazing: Australia's remote campsites, such as those in the Outback, offer exceptional stargazing opportunities, with minimal light pollution and crystal-clear skies.

Fishing and Water Activities: Coastal campsites often provide access to fishing, kayaking, and swimming in tranquil waters.

Types of Camping in Australia

Basic Campsites: Usually located in national parks, these offer limited facilities like fire pits, toilets, and picnic tables, perfect for self-sufficient campers.

Caravan Parks: Found near popular tourist spots, these sItes provide powered sites, hot showers, and communal kitchens, ideal for those seeking comfort.

Eco-Camping: Designed for sustainability, eco-campgrounds use renewable energy and have minimal environmental impact. Examples include **Bay of Fires Conservation Area** in Tasmania.

Wild Camping: In designated remote areas, wild camping lets you connect with untouched nature but requires adherence to local guidelines to protect the environment.

Essential Camping Tips

Plan Ahead: Book campsites in advance, especially in popular destinations during peak seasons.

Pack Appropriately: Bring weather-appropriate clothing, a sturdy tent, sleeping gear, and camping essentials such as a first-aid kit, flashlight, and portable stove.

Respect Wildlife: Observe animals from a distance and store food securely to avoid attracting them.

Follow Fire Regulations: Check local fire bans and use designated fire pits when allowed.

Leave No Trace: Dispose of waste responsibly and leave the campsite as you found it.

Stay Safe: Familiarize yourself with local hazards such as snakes, spiders, and changing weather conditions.

Cycling and Road Trips

Cycling Adventures

Australia's cycling trails vary from urban routes to challenging mountain paths, offering something for everyone—from casual riders to seasoned cyclists.

Top Cycling Trails

Great Ocean Road (Victoria): Cycle along this iconic coastal route with breathtaking ocean views, cliffs, and rainforests.

Centennial Parklands (Sydney): Perfect for families and beginners, this park features wide, well-maintained tracks.

Munda Biddi Trail (Western Australia): A world-class off-road cycling trail through stunning forests and tranquil countryside, stretching over 1,000 kilometers.

Mount Lofty Ranges (South Australia): Offers scenic hill climbs and panoramic views near Adelaide.

Tasmanian East Coast Trail (Tasmania): Explore picturesque beaches, quaint towns, and rolling hills in a relaxed setting.

Cycling Tips

- Wear protective gear, including a helmet (mandatory in Australia).
- Follow local cycling rules and stick to designated bike lanes.
- Carry a repair kit, water, and snacks for longer rides.
- Check weather conditions before setting out.

Road Trip Adventures

Australia's vast network of roads offers the freedom to explore its stunning and varied landscapes. From coastal drives to Outback adventures, road trips are a quintessential way to experience the country.

Epic Road Trip Routes

Great Ocean Road (Victoria): This world-famous route features landmarks like the Twelve Apostles, picturesque beaches, and lush rainforests.

Pacific Coast Drive (New South Wales to Queensland): Journey from Sydney to Brisbane, stopping at charming towns, beaches, and the Hunter Valley wine region.

Red Centre Way (Northern Territory): Venture through the heart of Australia, exploring Uluru, Kings Canyon, and Alice Springs.

Gibb River Road (Western Australia): A rugged Outback adventure through the Kimberley region, featuring gorges, waterfalls, and stunning vistas.

Tasmanian Circle Drive (Tasmania): Discover Tasmania's stunning coastlines, national parks, and historic sites on this compact island drive.

Key Road Trip Tips

- Plan your route and check road conditions, especially in remote areas.
- Carry extra fuel, water, and a spare tire for long journeys.
- Respect speed limits and watch out for wildlife, especially at dawn and dusk.
- Use rest areas to avoid fatigue during long drives.

Combining Cycling and Road Trips

Why not combine both adventures? Pack your bike and hit the road! Many road trip routes intersect with excellent cycling trails, allowing you to switch between driving and riding for a varied and exciting experience.

Example Combo Trip

Start with a road trip along the Great Ocean Road, stopping to cycle through sections like the Otway National Park or coastal towns for a closer look at their beauty.

Why It's Special

Cycling and road trips in Australia are more than just modes of travel—they are ways to connect with the country's rich natural and cultural landscapes. Whether you're pedaling through verdant trails or cruising along vast highways, every journey reveals new sights, sounds, and experiences.

Prepare your gear, plan your route, and set off on an unforgettable Australian adventure!

Indigenous Experiences and Cultural Tours

Top Indigenous Experiences

Uluru Cultural Tours (Northern Territory)

Learn about the spiritual significance of Uluru to the Anangu people. Guided tours, like those offered by the **Uluru-Kata Tjuta National Park**, include insights into Dreamtime stories, bush foods, and traditional art.

Kakadu National Park (Northern Territory)

Explore ancient rock art galleries at Ubirr and Nourlangie, some of which date back over 20,000 years. Engage with local guides who share stories of the land and its traditional owners.

Tjapukai Aboriginal Cultural Park (Queensland)

Near Cairns, this interactive experience showcases the customs, art, and music of the Tjapukai people. Activities include boomerang throwing, bush tucker tasting, and didgeridoo playing.

Bundyi Cultural Tours (New South Wales)

Join Wiradjuri guide Mark Saddler on personalized tours of the Riverina region, exploring significant sites, traditional practices, and Indigenous perspectives on the natural world.

Cultural Walking Tours in Sydney (New South Wales)

Discover the Gadigal land with tours like **Barangaroo Aboriginal Cultural Tours**, which highlight the importance of Sydney's harbor and its Indigenous heritage.

Mossman Gorge Centre (Queensland)

Guided by Kuku Yalanji people, this rainforest tour delves into bush medicine, traditional uses of plants, and Dreamtime stories of the Daintree Rainforest.

Tiwi Islands (Northern Territory)

Visit the Tiwi Islands, known as the "Island of Smiles," to experience their vibrant art scene, unique ceremonies, and friendly community life.

What to Expect

Storytelling and Dreamtime: Hear captivating tales of creation and the deep spiritual connections Indigenous people have with the land and its features.

Art and Craft Workshops: Participate in traditional art-making, dot painting, and weaving sessions.

Bush Tucker and Medicine: Learn about native foods, medicinal plants, and sustainable living practices.

Cultural Performances: Enjoy traditional dances, didgeridoo music, and ceremonial displays.

Hands-On Activities: Try boomerang or spear throwing, or learn about traditional hunting and fishing techniques.

Why Indigenous Experiences Matter

Participating in these tours fosters a respectful appreciation of the knowledge, resilience, and contributions of Australia's First Nations communities. These encounters not only enhance your travel experience but also support Indigenous-led tourism initiatives, helping preserve their culture and empower local communities.

Tips for a Meaningful Experience

Engage Respectfully: Listen attentively, ask thoughtful questions, and follow cultural protocols.

Book Authentic Tours: Choose operators that are Indigenous-owned or directly involve local communities.

Be Open-Minded: Approach experiences with curiosity and a willingness to learn.

Support Local Art and Crafts: Purchase souvenirs directly from Indigenous artists to ensure fair compensation.

Chapter 7: Australian Culture
Indigenous Culture and History

A Deep Connection to the Land

For Indigenous Australians, the land is more than a physical space—it is a living, sacred entity. Their custodianship reflects a sustainable way of life, preserving ecosystems through traditional ecological knowledge. This spiritual relationship is at the heart of Dreamtime, the foundation of their culture.

Dreamtime Stories: Passed down through generations, these tales explain the creation of the world, sacred sites, and the laws governing relationships between people and nature.

Significant Sites: Iconic locations like **Uluru**, **Kata Tjuta**, and the **Great Barrier Reef** hold deep spiritual significance and feature prominently in Indigenous lore.

Art and Storytelling

Indigenous art is a vibrant expression of their connection to the land and Dreamtime.

Dot Painting: A unique style originating in the Central and Western Desert regions, often depicting landscapes, animals, and Dreamtime stories.

Rock Art: Found in places like **Kakadu National Park**, these ancient paintings date back tens of thousands of years, providing insights into daily life, spiritual beliefs, and historical events.

Contemporary Art: Many Indigenous artists blend traditional techniques with modern styles, gaining recognition in global art markets.

Traditional Practices

Bush Tucker: Indigenous Australians have used native plants and animals for food, medicine, and tools for millennia. Today, bush foods like kangaroo, wattleseed, and lemon myrtle are celebrated in modern Australian cuisine.

Cultural Ceremonies: Songlines, dances, and rituals are integral to passing on knowledge, celebrating milestones, and maintaining community bonds.

Historical Challenges and Resilience

Australia's Indigenous peoples have faced immense challenges since European colonization in 1788, including dispossession, forced removal, and cultural suppression.

Stolen Generations: Between 1910 and 1970, many Indigenous children were forcibly taken from their families in an attempt to assimilate them into European culture.

Land Rights Movement: Efforts like the 1992 **Mabo Decision** have gradually recognized Indigenous ownership and connection to the land.

Cultural Revitalization: In recent decades, there has been a resurgence in celebrating and preserving Indigenous languages, traditions, and stories.

Why It Matters

Understanding Indigenous culture and history fosters respect, reconciliation, and a deeper appreciation for Australia's identity. Visiting cultural sites, participating in Indigenous-led tours, and supporting local communities are ways to connect meaningfully with this rich heritage.

By embracing and honoring Indigenous culture, you'll gain a profound insight into the land and its people, enriching your Australian journey.

Australian Cuisine and Food Culture

Indigenous Bush Foods

For thousands of years, Indigenous Australians relied on bush tucker—native plants and animals—for sustenance. These ingredients are now celebrated in contemporary cuisine.

Popular Bush Foods:

Kangaroo: A lean, high-protein meat with a unique flavor, often grilled or made into pies.

Wattleseed: Used in bread, desserts, and coffee for its nutty, roasted flavor.

Lemon Myrtle: A fragrant herb added to sauces, teas, and baked goods.

Quandong: A tart fruit used in jams and desserts.

Many modern chefs incorporate these ingredients to highlight Australia's Indigenous food heritage.

Iconic Australian Dishes

Meat Pies: A quintessential Aussie snack filled with minced meat and gravy. Best enjoyed at a local bakery or sporting event.

Vegemite on Toast: A savory spread made from yeast extract, often served with butter on toast.

Lamingtons: Sponge cakes coated in chocolate and coconut, a beloved dessert.

Pavlova: A meringue-based dessert topped with fresh fruits, often claimed as Australia's national dish.

Barramundi: A prized fish served grilled or pan-fried, symbolizing Australia's love for fresh seafood.

Multicultural Influence

Australia's immigrant history has enriched its culinary landscape, introducing flavors from around the world.

Asian Influence: Cities like Sydney and Melbourne are renowned for their authentic Thai, Vietnamese, and Chinese cuisine.

Mediterranean Fare: Greek souvlaki, Italian pasta, and Lebanese falafel are widely popular.

Fusion Cuisine: Chefs creatively combine global techniques and native ingredients, resulting in unique dishes like kangaroo burgers or wattleseed ice cream.

Seafood Delights

Surrounded by oceans, Australia boasts an abundance of fresh seafood.

Prawns and Lobsters: Often grilled for a classic Aussie barbecue.

Oysters: Best enjoyed fresh from regions like Coffin Bay in South Australia.

Moreton Bay Bugs: A type of flat lobster, often served with garlic butter.

Cafe Culture

Australia's cafe scene is world-class, with coffee culture at its core.

Flat White: A signature Australian coffee, similar to a latte but with less foam.

Brunch Favorites: Avocado toast, poached eggs, and bircher muesli are staples.

Wine and Craft Beer

Australia is home to internationally acclaimed wine regions like Barossa Valley, Hunter Valley, and Margaret River. Pairing wine with local cuisine is a must-try experience. Additionally, the craft beer scene is booming, offering unique flavors from small breweries nationwide.

Why It's Special

Australian cuisine reflects the country's diversity, creativity, and deep respect for its natural resources. From bush-inspired dishes to international flavors, every bite tells a story of tradition, innovation, and multicultural harmony. Whether dining in a fine restaurant, enjoying a backyard barbecue, or exploring local markets, Australia's food culture is sure to leave you with unforgettable flavors.

Festivals and Events

Major National Festivals

Australia Day (January 26)

A national holiday marking the arrival of the First Fleet in 1788. Celebrations include barbecues, fireworks, parades, and cultural events across the country.

ANZAC Day (April 25)

A day of remembrance for Australians and New Zealanders who served in wars. Dawn services and marches honor their legacy, with a solemn yet unifying atmosphere.

Christmas and New Year's Eve

Australians celebrate Christmas with summer beach parties and barbecues. New Year's Eve features spectacular fireworks, especially in Sydney, with the iconic Harbour Bridge display.

Music and Arts Festivals

Sydney Festival (January)

A multi-arts extravaganza featuring theatre, dance, music, and visual arts, held in venues across Sydney.

Splendour in the Grass (July)

One of Australia's premier music festivals, held in Byron Bay, showcasing international and local artists across multiple genres.

Adelaide Fringe (February–March)

The largest arts festival in the Southern Hemisphere, offering comedy, cabaret, theatre, and visual arts in a lively, inclusive atmosphere.

Melbourne International Comedy Festival (March–April)

A world-renowned comedy event featuring stand-up acts, improvisation, and satire from top performers worldwide.

Food and Wine Festivals

Taste of Tasmania (December–January)

Tasmania's premier food festival, showcasing the island's exceptional produce, wines, and artisanal goods.

Barossa Vintage Festival (April)

A celebration of the Barossa Valley's wine heritage, with tastings, vineyard tours, and culinary events.

Noosa Food and Wine Festival (May)

Held on Queensland's Sunshine Coast, this event highlights the region's fresh seafood, local wines, and gourmet delights.

Cultural and Indigenous Festivals

Garma Festival (August)

Held in Arnhem Land, Northern Territory, this is Australia's leading Indigenous cultural festival, featuring traditional music, art, and storytelling.

National Multicultural Festival (February)

Celebrated in Canberra, this event brings together cultures from around the world through food, performances, and workshops.

Dreamtime at the 'G (September)

A celebration of Aboriginal and Torres Strait Islander culture during an Australian Rules football match in Melbourne.

Sporting Events

Australian Open (January)

One of tennis's four Grand Slam tournaments, hosted in Melbourne.

Melbourne Cup (November)

Australia's most famous horse race, known as "the race that stops the nation."

Sydney to Hobart Yacht Race (December 26)

A thrilling ocean race starting in Sydney and finishing in Tasmania, attracting competitors and spectators from around the globe.

Why Attend Australian Festivals?

Festivals In Australia offer a chance to experience the country's vibrant personality. They provide a platform to connect with locals, savor regional specialties, and enjoy world-class performances. Whether you're drawn to cultural traditions, culinary delights, or lively music, Australian events promise unforgettable memories.

Sports and Recreation

Popular Sports in Australia

Australian Rules Football (AFL)

Often called "footy," AFL is uniquely Australian and draws massive crowds, particularly in Melbourne. Attending a match at the Melbourne Cricket Ground (MCG) is a must for sports lovers.

Cricket
Cricket is a national pastime, with major events like the Boxing Day Test and the Big Bash League attracting fans of all ages.

Rugby
Both Rugby League and Rugby Union are widely played, with the State of Origin series being a highlight on the sports calendar.

Tennis
The Australian Open, held annually in Melbourne, is one of the four Grand Slam tournaments and a global showcase of tennis talent.

Soccer (Football)

Soccer continues to grow in popularity, with the A-League and international matches drawing enthusiastic crowds.

Water-Based Recreation

Surfing

Australia's iconic beaches, like Bondi, Bells Beach, and Byron Bay, make it a paradise for surfers. Whether you're a pro or a beginner, there's a wave for you.

Swimming and Snorkeling

Crystal-clear waters and vibrant reefs invite visitors to swim and snorkel, especially at hotspots like the Great Barrier Reef and Ningaloo Reef.

Kayaking and Paddleboarding

Explore Australia's stunning coastlines, rivers, and lakes through these popular activities, ideal for enjoying the country's natural beauty.

Fishing

From deep-sea fishing to casting a line in tranquil rivers, Australia is a top destination for anglers.

Land-Based Activities

Hiking and Bushwalking

Explore breathtaking landscapes through trails like the Overland Track in Tasmania or the Blue Mountains near Sydney.

Cycling

With scenic routes like the Great Ocean Road and urban bike paths, Australia is perfect for both casual and avid cyclists.

Golf

World-class golf courses, including Royal Melbourne and Barnbougle Dunes, attract players seeking stunning backdrops and challenging greens.

Rock Climbing

Test your skills at iconic locations like the Grampians in Victoria or the Glass House Mountains in Queensland.

Recreational Highlights

Beach Culture

Beaches are central to Australian recreation, offering opportunities for sunbathing, picnics, beach volleyball, and more.

National Parks

Discover Australia's diverse ecosystems through activities like wildlife spotting, camping, and guided eco-tours in parks such as Kakadu and Daintree.

Extreme Sports

Thrill-seekers can enjoy activities like skydiving, bungee jumping, and zip-lining in adventure hubs such as Cairns and Queenstown.

The Arts and Music Scene

Art and Visual Arts

Indigenous Art

Indigenous Australian art is one of the oldest continuous art traditions in the world. Visitors can explore ancient rock art sites, such as those in Kakadu National Park, or experience modern Indigenous artworks in galleries like the National Gallery of Australia in Canberra. Aboriginal dot painting and traditional bark painting remain integral to Australia's artistic expression.

Contemporary Art

Australia has a thriving contemporary art scene, with cities like Melbourne, Sydney, and Brisbane hosting numerous galleries and exhibitions. The Art Gallery of New South Wales and the National Gallery of Victoria showcase both local and international contemporary artists, while Sydney's Biennale and Melbourne's NGV Triennial draw attention to cutting-edge works.

Public Art

Australia is known for its impressive public art installations, from the colorful laneways of Melbourne to the large-scale sculptures along Sydney's Circular Quay. Street art, particularly in Melbourne, is considered some of the best in the world, with entire neighborhoods dedicated to murals and graffiti art.

Music and Performance

Live Music

Australia is a hotspot for live music, with cities like Sydney and Melbourne offering a wide variety of venues, from intimate clubs to large concert halls. Iconic venues include the Sydney Opera House, which hosts both classical and contemporary performances, and Melbourne's The Forum Theatre, known for its historic beauty and excellent acoustics.

Festivals

Music festivals play a key role in Australia's musical culture. From the eclectic **Splendour in the Grass** in Byron Bay to the electronic beats of **Rainbow Serpent** in Victoria, the festival scene attracts international and local talent. Additionally, **Bluesfest** and **Falls Festival** offer a wide array of genres from folk and blues to indie rock.

Opera and Classical Music

The **Sydney Opera House** is not only a world-renowned architectural marvel but also a hub for operatic and classical music performances. **Opera Australia** stages numerous productions throughout the year, while the **Melbourne Symphony Orchestra** and the **Sydney Symphony Orchestra** offer regular classical music concerts.

Indigenous Music

The influence of Indigenous music is prominent in Australia's cultural identity. Traditional instruments like the didgeridoo and clapsticks are commonly featured in performances, alongside contemporary Indigenous musicians who fuse traditional sounds with modern genres. The **Garma Festival** in Arnhem Land celebrates the music, song, and dance of the Yolŋu people.

Theatre and Dance

Theatre

Australia has a rich theatrical tradition, with performances spanning from classic works to cutting-edge contemporary productions. Major theatre companies include **Belvoir St Theatre** in Sydney, **Melbourne Theatre Company**, and **Malthouse Theatre** in Melbourne. These venues often showcase Australian playwrights, as well as international works.

Dance

Dance is an integral part of Australian performing arts. The **Australian Ballet**, based in Melbourne, is internationally renowned, while companies like **Bangarra Dance Theatre** blend contemporary dance with Indigenous storytelling. Dance festivals like **Melbourne Dance Week** showcase local and international talent.

Why Australia's Arts and Music Scene Matters

Australia's arts and music scene is a vital part of its national identity, offering a platform for both Indigenous and contemporary expressions. With a rich mix of cultural influences, Australian art and music offer something for every taste, from traditional Indigenous performances to avant-garde theatre and world-class music festivals.

Chapter 8: Shopping in Australia
Souvenirs and Indigenous Crafts

Indigenous Crafts

Aboriginal Art

Aboriginal art is one of Australia's most iconic and enduring souvenirs. Traditional Indigenous artworks, often created using dot painting techniques, depict Dreamtime stories and the connection between land, culture, and spirituality. Popular items include painted canvases, boomerangs, and bark paintings, many of which are made by Indigenous artists from remote communities. The **National Gallery of Australia** and the **Art Gallery of New South Wales** offer a wide selection, and many galleries and cultural centers in towns like Alice Springs and Broome feature original pieces for sale.

Didgeridoos

The didgeridoo is one of the most recognizable Indigenous instruments and a popular souvenir. Handcrafted from wood, often eucalyptus, these instruments are traditionally played by Aboriginal people of northern Australia. When purchasing a didgeridoo, it's important to ensure it's made in an ethical and sustainable way, often through Indigenous-owned cooperatives or local artisans.

Bark Art and Carvings

Bark art involves painting on sheets of bark from native trees, with intricate designs that often tell stories of the artist's cultural heritage. Carvings made from wood, such as animals, faces, or spirit figures, are also highly sought after. These pieces are deeply symbolic and often represent ancestral connections to the land.

Clapsticks

Used in traditional Aboriginal ceremonies and performances, clapsticks are another significant item to bring back from your travels. They are often made from hardwood and hand-carved with intricate patterns, each one telling a unique story.

Australian Souvenirs

Opals

Known as Australia's national gemstone, opals are found in regions like Coober

Pedy and Lightning Ridge. They are famous for their unique play of color, which makes them a perfect keepsake. Opals are commonly used in jewelry, ranging from rings and necklaces to earrings and pendants, making them both a beautiful and memorable souvenir.

Australian Wool Products

Australia's wool industry is world-renowned, and products like scarves, blankets, and jumpers made from high-quality Australian merino wool make great souvenirs. They are perfect for both warmth and as luxury keepsakes.

Timber Products

Handcrafted wooden items such as coasters, bowls, and cutting boards made from Australian hardwood are popular souvenirs. These products highlight the country's stunning natural resources and showcase the craftsmanship of local artisans.

Local Food and Wine

Bringing back a bottle of Australian wine from the renowned vineyards in regions like Barossa Valley or Hunter Valley is a great way to remember your trip. Australian wines, particularly Shiraz and Chardonnay, are famous worldwide. Other food-based souvenirs include native Australian spices, bush honey, and gourmet chocolate.

Aussie Apparel

Australia is home to several iconic fashion brands, many of which offer high-quality clothing and accessories that represent the country's laid-back style. Brands like R.M. Williams, Akubra hats, and UGG boots are staples of Australian fashion that make for excellent souvenirs, combining practicality with style.

Where to Find Indigenous Crafts and Souvenirs

Indigenous Art Galleries

Across Australia, galleries in cities like Melbourne, Sydney, and Alice Springs offer authentic Indigenous artworks and crafts. The **National Indigenous Art Gallery** in Canberra and the **Aboriginal Art and Culture Centre** in Broome are excellent places to find both traditional and contemporary pieces.

Markets and Festivals

Many local markets feature Indigenous artisans selling handcrafted goods. The **Eumundi Markets** in Queensland, **The Rocks Markets** in Sydney, and **Fremantle Markets** in Perth showcase Indigenous arts alongside other Australian-made crafts.

Cultural Centers

Many cultural centers in Indigenous communities, such as the **Tjapukai Cultural Park** in Cairns or the **Kakadu National Park Visitor Centre**, offer handmade crafts and art that support local Indigenous artists. Purchasing items from these centers ensures that profits go back to the community.

Markets and Flea Markets

Popular Markets Across Australia

Queen Victoria Market (Melbourne)

One of the largest open-air markets in the Southern Hemisphere, **Queen Victoria Market** is a must-visit for any traveler in Melbourne. Known for its fresh food stalls, artisanal products, and vibrant atmosphere, this historic market is the place to go for local produce, meats, cheeses, and gourmet foods. Don't miss the **Night Markets** in summer, which offer a mix of street food, live music, and art.

The Rocks Market (Sydney)

Located in the heart of Sydney, **The Rocks Market** offers a combination of handcrafted jewelry, unique art, fashion, and homeware from local artists and designers. It's a great place to find one-of-a-kind souvenirs and gifts. On weekends, the market bustles with performers, artisans, and food vendors, making it an ideal spot to spend an afternoon.

Fremantle Markets (Perth)

Situated in the historic Fremantle district, **Fremantle Markets** is a lively and colorful market offering a diverse range of goods. Known for its arts and crafts stalls, fresh produce, and food offerings, this market is a vibrant mix of cultures. It's also home to some of Perth's most unique and locally made products, including Indigenous art, handmade jewelry, and organic skincare.

Eumundi Markets (Queensland)

Located in the Sunshine Coast hinterland, **Eumundi Markets** is one of Australia's most famous artisan markets. A hub for handmade and sustainable goods, it offers everything from bohemian clothing to original artwork, homemade jams, and freshly brewed coffee. The market is also known for its live music and street performances, adding to the laid-back atmosphere of the area.

South Melbourne Market (Melbourne)

A favorite for food lovers, **South Melbourne Market** is renowned for its seafood, deli items, and artisanal food stalls. Whether you're seeking fresh fish, cheeses, local wines, or homemade baked goods, this market has it all. It's also a great place to grab some gourmet ingredients if you're planning a picnic or cooking your own meal while in town.

Paddington Markets (Sydney)

Located in the fashionable suburb of Paddington, **Paddington Markets** is known for its stylish fashion offerings, vintage finds, and high-quality handcrafted goods. The market has a boutique atmosphere with a focus on local fashion designers, jewelry makers, and artists. It's an excellent place to pick up a unique souvenir or an original piece of Australian art or fashion.

Carriageworks Farmers Market (Sydney)

If you're in Sydney and looking for fresh, organic produce, **Carriageworks Farmers Market** is the place to go. Held weekly, this market offers a selection of locally grown fruits, vegetables, meats, and cheeses. It's a great spot for foodies who want to experience the freshest local produce and sample artisanal foods from small Australian producers.

What to Expect at Australian Flea Markets

Vintage Clothing and Collectibles

Australian flea markets are a great place to hunt for vintage clothing, retro items, and collectible goods. Whether it's an old vinyl record, classic furniture, or unique clothing pieces from decades past, flea markets across the country offer an exciting range of nostalgic items.

Antiques and Curiosities

Some of Australia's larger flea markets feature antique stalls where you can find everything from rare books to vintage toys, fine china, and old tools. These markets offer a fascinating mix of historical treasures and quirky oddities, making it an adventure in itself to explore each stall.

Local Handmade Goods

In addition to vintage finds, Australian flea markets often have a selection of locally handmade goods. You'll find art, craft items, custom furniture, jewelry, and home décor created by local artisans. It's an ideal place to purchase a special, handmade souvenir that reflects Australia's creative spirit.

Street Food and Snacks

Many of Australia's markets, including flea markets, feature food trucks and vendors selling delicious street food. From local delicacies like meat pies and sausage rolls to international flavors such as tacos, dumplings, and falafel, the food at these markets is as much a draw as the shopping.

Where to Find Flea Markets in Australia

Camberwell Market (Melbourne)

Known for its large selection of secondhand goods, **Camberwell Market** is a popular flea market in Melbourne. Shoppers can find everything from vintage clothing to retro furniture, books, and bric-a-brac. The market is also home to a selection of gourmet food stalls, making it a great way to spend a Saturday afternoon.

Sydney's Glebe Markets

Located in the inner-west of Sydney, **Glebe Markets** is known for its eclectic mix of vintage fashion, retro items, and secondhand goods. With a focus on sustainability, you'll also find plenty of locally-made and upcycled items. It's the perfect place for bargain hunters and vintage lovers.

Brisbane's Collective Markets

Held in South Bank, the **Collective Markets** in Brisbane offer a mix of arts, crafts, and vintage items. Whether you're looking for handmade jewelry, art, or a unique gift, the Collective Markets offer a wide range of treasures. You'll also find plenty of street food options to refuel while you shop.

Adelaide's Gilles Street Market

Known for its trendy, alternative vibe, **Gilles Street Market** in Adelaide offers a wide selection of secondhand goods, handmade items, and unique finds. This market is particularly popular with locals looking for cool vintage clothing, accessories, and artwork. It's an ideal spot to hunt for something offbeat and original.

Tips for Shopping at Australian Markets and Flea Markets

Bargaining: Some markets, especially flea markets, allow bargaining, so don't hesitate to negotiate prices, especially when purchasing multiple items.

Arrive Early: Arriving early gives you the best chance of finding unique items before they sell out. It also allows you to enjoy the market before it gets too crowded.

Cash: While many markets accept cards, it's still a good idea to carry cash, especially at smaller or more remote markets.

Wear Comfortable Shoes: Markets can be large and require plenty of walking, so comfortable shoes are a must.

Plan to Spend Time: Markets are a great way to soak up the local atmosphere, so allow yourself plenty of time to explore and chat with vendors.

Luxury Shopping

Top Luxury Shopping Destinations

Sydney - The Ultimate Shopping Hub

Sydney is a major global city with a flourishing luxury shopping scene. **Pitt Street Mall** is a prime location for high-end fashion, with flagship stores from luxury brands like **Gucci**, **Louis Vuitton**, **Prada**, and **Chanel**. **The Strand Arcade** is another hotspot, offering a more boutique luxury shopping experience, with stores like **Mimco** and **Alex Perry**. **Westfield Sydney** also features an extensive collection of luxury labels, along with designer jewelry and fine watches.

Melbourne - A Fashion Capital

Melbourne is known for its eclectic mix of high-end fashion, art, and design. **Collins Street**, often referred to as the "Paris End" of Melbourne, is where you'll find top designer boutiques, including **Dior**, **Saint Laurent**, **Hermès**, and **Chanel**. The **Royal Arcade** and **Block Arcade** are historic shopping precincts that offer a selection of luxury brands, as well as unique jewelry shops and exclusive Australian designers. Melbourne's luxury shopping scene also includes **Chadstone Shopping Centre**, the largest shopping center in the Southern Hemisphere, with an impressive collection of international luxury retailers.

Brisbane - Upscale Fashion and Style

Brisbane's **Queen Street Mall** is home to a number of designer boutiques and luxury stores. For a more exclusive shopping experience, head to **James Street**, an upscale shopping precinct featuring high-end Australian designers like **Zimmermann**, **Saba**, and **Cameo Collective**, along with international brands such as **Loewe** and **Tiffany & Co**. Brisbane also boasts **Westfield Carindale**, which has a selection of luxury goods, from fashion to jewelry.

The Gold Coast - Coastal Luxury

The Gold Coast offers a relaxed yet refined shopping experience. **Pacific Fair Shopping Centre** is the largest shopping center in Queensland, and features an array of luxury retailers, including **Fendi**, **Burberry**, and **Chanel**. For a more boutique experience, explore **The 4217**, a luxury shopping precinct in Surfers Paradise, offering designer clothing, fine jewelry, and art galleries.

Adelaide - Elegant and Refined

Adelaide's **Rundle Mall** is home to several high-end stores, including **Louis Vuitton**, **Gucci**, and **Dior**. The city's **King William Road** offers a mix of luxury boutiques and specialty stores, making it an excellent spot for those seeking unique designer items. Adelaide is also known for its fine wine and gourmet food, making it the perfect destination for combining shopping with food and wine experiences.

Luxury Fashion and Designers

Zimmermann

One of Australia's most celebrated luxury fashion brands, **Zimmermann** is known for its elegant and feminine designs, blending contemporary styles with vintage-inspired elements. Its high-end clothing, swimwear, and accessories are often seen on celebrities and have become synonymous with luxury and style. Zimmermann boutiques can be found in major Australian cities like Sydney and Melbourne.

Kendall + Kylie

The **Kendall + Kylie** brand, founded by the Jenner sisters, is a prominent luxury fashion label that offers high-end footwear, handbags, and accessories. The label has become popular in Australia, known for its edgy yet glamorous designs.

Aje

Aje is an Australian fashion label that focuses on luxury with a bohemian twist. Known for its distinctive silhouettes and unique prints, Aje's collections have earned a loyal following both in Australia and abroad. The brand offers beautifully crafted dresses, tops, and accessories, perfect for any occasion.

R.M. Williams

While often associated with country wear, **R.M. Williams** has become a luxury brand in Australia thanks to its premium craftsmanship. The brand's iconic leather boots, along with stylish jackets, shirts, and accessories, represent the very best of Australian craftsmanship and are a luxury in their own right.

Jewelry and Watches

Australia's luxury shopping isn't limited to fashion—fine jewelry and luxury watches are also highly sought after. **Paspaley Pearls**, based in Perth, is one of the world's leading pearl companies, offering high-quality pearls that are often regarded as some of the finest in the world. If you're looking for luxury watches, **Omega** and **Rolex** are available in Australian cities like Sydney and Melbourne, offering timepieces with global prestige.

Luxury Australian Beauty Brands

For those seeking luxurious skincare and beauty products, **Aesop** is one of Australia's top luxury brands, known for its high-quality botanical skincare, body care, and fragrances. The brand's chic stores can be found across the country, offering an array of luxurious products in minimalist packaging.

Best Shopping Districts

1. Sydney – The Fashion Capital

Pitt Street Mall: Known as the heart of Sydney's retail scene, **Pitt Street Mall** is lined with global luxury brands, department stores, and major Australian labels. Here you'll find **Louis Vuitton**, **Gucci**, **Prada**, and **Chanel**, along with popular retailers like **Apple** and **Zara**.

Queen Victoria Building (QVB): This iconic Victorian-era building offers a refined shopping experience with a mix of luxury brands, including **Rolex**, **BOSS**, and **Kate Spade**, alongside unique boutiques. The QVB also has a fantastic selection of cafes for a break from shopping.

The Rocks: Known for its historic charm, **The Rocks** features local markets, artisanal products, and boutique stores selling handmade crafts, jewelry, and unique souvenirs. It's perfect for finding something one-of-a-kind.

2. Melbourne – A Stylish Blend of High-End and Indie Shops

Collins Street (Paris End): Collins Street, often referred to as Melbourne's "Paris End," is home to an impressive range of designer boutiques and luxury stores, including **Louis Vuitton**, **Dior**, and **Chanel**. For fashion enthusiasts, it's a must-visit destination.

Chadstone Shopping Centre: As the largest shopping center in the Southern Hemisphere, **Chadstone** offers an extensive selection of international and local luxury retailers, including **Fendi**, **Burberry**, and **Prada**, making it a top choice for high-end shopping.

Fitzroy and Brunswick Street: For a more eclectic shopping experience, **Fitzroy** offers a mix of independent boutiques, vintage shops, and local designers. It's the ideal spot for those looking for unique, one-of-a-kind clothing, jewelry, and art.

3. Brisbane – Upscale Shopping in a Laid-Back Setting

Queen Street Mall: Brisbane's **Queen Street Mall** is a bustling retail hub with a variety of stores ranging from major department stores to designer boutiques. You'll find high-end brands like **Coach**, **Lacoste**, and **Burberry**, along with popular chains and specialty shops.

James Street: Known for its chic, upscale atmosphere, **James Street** in the Fortitude Valley offers a blend of high-end fashion, art galleries, homewares, and contemporary Australian brands like **Zimmermann**, **Saba**, and **Cameo Collective**.

Eagle Street Pier: This riverside area features a mix of fine dining, local artisan shops, and unique boutiques selling fashion, art, and home decor. It's perfect for a more relaxed shopping experience by the water.

4. Gold Coast – Luxury Meets Coastal Style

Pacific Fair Shopping Centre: Located in Broadbeach, **Pacific Fair** is the Gold Coast's largest shopping center, offering everything from international luxury brands like **Chanel**, **Fendi**, and **Gucci** to contemporary Australian designers.

The 4217: This boutique shopping precinct in Surfers Paradise is known for its luxury stores, including fashion, art galleries, and homeware stores, offering a more intimate shopping experience in a coastal setting.

Broadbeach Mall: For a more laid-back shopping experience, **Broadbeach Mall** offers local boutiques, beachwear, and casual fashion, making it perfect for picking up souvenirs or finding a stylish beach outfit.

5. Adelaide – Luxury with a Touch of Heritage

Rundle Mall: **Rundle Mall** is Adelaide's main shopping street, offering a mix of department stores, fashion boutiques, and luxury brands like **Louis Vuitton**, **Gucci**, and **David Jones**. It's the go-to shopping destination for both high-end items and everyday fashion.

King William Road: For a more refined shopping experience, **King William Road** offers a range of upscale boutiques selling Australian designer brands, homeware, and art. It's a quieter shopping area, perfect for those seeking a more relaxed, boutique-style shopping experience.

Glenelg: Located near the beach, **Glenelg** is a lively shopping area that combines coastal charm with a variety of stores, from fashion boutiques to local jewelry designers. The nearby beach makes it a great place for shopping and relaxation.

6. Perth – Urban Style Meets Coastal Living

King Street: Known as Perth's luxury retail precinct, **King Street** is home to exclusive designer boutiques, including **Chanel**, **Louis Vuitton**, and **BOSS**. The street is also known for its high-end art galleries and fine jewelry stores.

Hay Street Mall: For a broader shopping experience, **Hay Street Mall** offers a mix of chain stores, local boutiques, and department stores. It's perfect for shoppers looking for variety, including Australian brands and international labels.

Claremont Quarter: For a more upscale suburban experience, **Claremont Quarter** is an elegant shopping center offering high-end fashion and beauty stores, with a selection of both Australian and international luxury retailers.

Chapter 9: Food and Dining
Australian Cuisine: What to Try

1. **Meat Pies**

Meat pies are a beloved and iconic snack in Australian cuisine, often considered a staple of Aussie comfort food. This handheld savory pastry is widely enjoyed across the country, from busy city streets to quiet rural towns. With its flaky golden crust and hearty filling, the meat pie is more than just food—it's a part of Australia's cultural identity, frequently found at bakeries, cafes, and sporting events.

Main Ingredients

The traditional Australian meat pie is made with a combination of the following key ingredients:

Meat: Beef, lamb, or chicken are common, though variations can include kangaroo or other meats.

Gravy: A rich, flavorful gravy is used to bind the meat filling and add moisture.

Vegetables: Common additions include onions, peas, and carrots.

Spices: Seasonings such as salt, pepper, and herbs are used to enhance the flavor.

The filling is encased in a buttery, flaky pastry, creating the perfect balance of texture and taste.

Where to Try in Australia

You can find meat pies almost anywhere in Australia, from local bakeries to upscale eateries. Some renowned spots to try them include:

Harry's Café de Wheels (Sydney): Famous for their iconic pie offerings, Harry's Café de Wheels is a must-visit for meat pie enthusiasts.

The Meat Pie Shop (Melbourne): Known for serving gourmet pies with a variety of fillings, including traditional and more adventurous options.

Bendigo's Bakery (Victoria): A local favorite offering fresh, delicious meat pies with multiple variations.

Bakers Delight (Australia-wide): A popular bakery chain that offers an assortment of meat pies across the country.

Taste

Meat pies deliver a comforting and satisfying taste with each bite. The rich, savory filling paired with the flaky pastry provides a delightful contrast of textures. The meat is tender and moist, while the gravy adds a depth of flavor, making it a perfect meal on the go. Depending on the type of meat used, the flavor profile can vary, with beef pies being heartier and lamb pies offering a unique, earthy taste.

What Makes It Special?

The meat pie is not just about flavor—it's deeply ingrained in Australian culture. It's a food that symbolizes simplicity and convenience, easily enjoyed while on the move or as part of a casual meal. The versatile fillings and endless variations mean that no two pies are exactly the same. Plus, meat pies are often enjoyed during significant Australian events, such as sporting games, where they hold a sense of nostalgia and community spirit. The ease of customization—whether topped with sauce, mashed potatoes, or served with chips—adds to its universal appeal.

Tips for Enjoying

Pair it with tomato sauce: Many Australians enjoy their meat pies with a generous squeeze of tomato sauce for added tanginess.

Try a "pie floater": In South Australia, a pie floater is a popular variation, where the pie is served on top of a bowl of pea soup. It's a fun twist on the traditional meat pie experience.

Choose a local bakery: While chain bakeries are widely available, trying a local, independent bakery often gives you a more authentic, homemade flavor.

Eat it with a side: Many Australians enjoy their pies with chips (fries) or a salad for a more filling meal.

Enjoy it with a cold beverage: Pair your meat pie with a chilled beer or a soft drink to complete your Aussie experience.

2. Vegemite on Toast

Vegemite on toast is a simple yet iconic Australian dish, widely considered a breakfast staple and a cultural symbol. Known for its unique, savory flavor, Vegemite is a dark brown spread made from yeast extract, enriched with B vitamins. Though its taste may be an acquired one, Australians grow up enjoying Vegemite on toast, making it a nostalgic and cherished dish for many. For visitors, it's a quintessential experience that offers a glimpse into the Australian palate.

Main Ingredients

The dish requires only a few basic components:

Vegemite: The star ingredient, a concentrated yeast extract spread.

Bread: Often white or wholemeal bread, toasted to perfection.

Butter or Margarine: Used as a base to soften the sharpness of Vegemite and make spreading easier.

Where to Try in Australia

Vegemite on toast can be found in nearly every Australian household and is commonly served at cafes and diners. Popular spots include:

Local Cafes: Many cafes across cities like Sydney and Melbourne serve it as part of a traditional breakfast menu.

Hotels and Hostels: Australian accommodations often include Vegemite on toast in their breakfast buffets.

Airport Lounges: Perfect for visitors eager to try it as soon as they arrive or before departure.

For the most authentic experience, try it at a casual local eatery or prepare it yourself from supplies at a grocery store.

Taste

Vegemite has a bold, salty, umami flavor that can surprise first-time tasters. When spread thinly on buttery toast, the saltiness is balanced by the richness of the butter and the crispness of the bread. The result is a savory, slightly tangy bite with a distinct taste that lingers, loved by many Australians.

What Makes It Special?

Cultural Icon: Vegemite is uniquely Australian and has been a part of the country's culinary identity since 1923.

Health Benefits: Packed with B vitamins like B1, B2, and B3, it's considered a healthy choice for boosting energy and metabolism.

Versatility: While toast is the most popular way to enjoy it, Vegemite is also used in sandwiches, crackers, or even recipes like stews and marinades.

Acquired Taste: Its bold flavor creates a love-it-or-hate-it reaction, making it a memorable culinary adventure for tourists.

Tips for Enjoying

Start Small: First-timers should apply a very thin layer of Vegemite to avoid being overwhelmed by its strong flavor.

Butter Generously: Spread a thick layer of butter or margarine first to mellow the sharpness of Vegemite.

Pair with Tea or Coffee: A hot beverage complements the savory taste and enhances the experience.

Experiment: Try variations like adding avocado slices or cheese on top for a unique twist.

Eat Like a Local: Observe how Australians spread their Vegemite, and don't hesitate to ask for tips!

3. Tim Tams

Tim Tams are a beloved Australian biscuit that has captured the hearts of locals and visitors alike. Made by Arnott's, these chocolate-coated biscuits consist of two layers of crunchy malted cookies sandwiched with a creamy chocolate filling, then covered in a smooth layer of chocolate. Often described as indulgent and irresistible, Tim Tams are a quintessential Australian snack, perfect for any time of day.

Main Ingredients

Biscuit Layers: Made from malted flour, sugar, and a hint of cocoa for a crisp texture.

Chocolate Cream Filling: A velvety chocolate ganache that provides a rich and creamy contrast.

Chocolate Coating: A smooth layer of milk, dark, or white chocolate that encases the biscuit.

Where to Try in Australia

Tim Tams are readily available across Australia at:

Supermarkets: Coles, Woolworths, and IGA stock a wide variety of Tim Tam flavors.

Convenience Stores: Perfect for picking up a quick treat while exploring.

Specialty Shops: Some high-end chocolate stores feature gourmet versions of Tim Tams.

For a fun experience, visit Arnott's Café or a local cafe offering Tim Tams paired with coffee or desserts.

Taste

Tim Tams deliver a luxurious mix of flavors and textures. The biscuit layers are slightly crunchy, the filling is smooth and creamy, and the chocolate coating melts in your mouth. The combination creates a perfect balance of sweetness, richness, and crunch, making every bite delightful.

What Makes It Special?

Cultural Significance: Tim Tams are an Aussie classic, often shared during tea breaks, gatherings, or as a gift.

Tim Tam Slam: A unique way to enjoy Tim Tams involves biting off the ends, using the biscuit as a straw to sip hot beverages like tea, coffee, or hot chocolate.

Flavor Variety: Beyond the classic milk chocolate, Tim Tams come in a range of flavors, including caramel, mint, white chocolate, and limited-edition creations.

Global Appeal: Though exported to other countries, the Australian-made versions remain the most authentic and sought-after.

Tips for Enjoying

Try the Tim Tam Slam: Bite off both ends, dip one into your hot drink, and sip through the biscuit like a straw—it's a warm, gooey delight!

Chill Them: Place Tim Tams in the refrigerator for a cooler, firmer texture.

Pair with Drinks: Enjoy with coffee, tea, or a glass of milk to complement their sweetness.

Gift Them: Tim Tams make an excellent souvenir for friends and family back home.

Explore Flavors: Sample different varieties to find your favorite or mix them into desserts like cheesecakes or milkshakes.

4. Barramundi

Barramundi, a prized fish in Australian cuisine, is synonymous with the country's love for fresh and flavorful seafood. Known for its mild, buttery taste and delicate texture, it's a versatile ingredient featured in various dishes, from fine dining menus to casual beachside grills. The name "barramundi" originates from the Aboriginal language, meaning "large-scaled river fish," and it is found in Australia's tropical and subtropical waters. Whether grilled, baked, or pan-fried, barramundi offers a quintessential Australian culinary experience.

Main Ingredients

The star of the dish is the barramundi itself, often complemented by:

Herbs and Spices: Thyme, parsley, lemon zest, or garlic to enhance its flavor.

Citrus: Lemon or lime for a refreshing touch.

Accompaniments: Commonly paired with roasted vegetables, salads, or mashed potatoes.

Where to Try in Australia

Barramundi is widely available at seafood restaurants, cafes, and markets across Australia. Top places to enjoy it include:

Cairns and Port Douglas: Restaurants near the Great Barrier Reef offer fresh, locally caught barramundi.

Darwin: Known for its barramundi fishing industry, Darwin offers it in a variety of styles.

Sydney and Melbourne: Upscale seafood restaurants and casual beachside eateries serve barramundi as a signature dish.

Fish Markets: Visit iconic markets like the Sydney Fish Market to buy fresh barramundi and cook it yourself.

Taste

Barramundi's flavor profile is mild yet rich, with a slightly sweet and nutty undertone. Its flesh is moist and flaky, making it appealing to those who enjoy a delicate and less "fishy" taste. The fish absorbs marinades and seasonings well, allowing chefs to create diverse dishes with bold or subtle flavors.

What Makes It Special?

Sustainability: Barramundi is a sustainable choice, often farmed responsibly in Australia to meet high environmental standards.

Versatility: Its mild flavor makes it suitable for various cooking methods, from grilling and baking to steaming and frying.

Health Benefits: High in omega-3 fatty acids and low in mercury, barramundi is a healthy seafood option.

Cultural Connection: The fish has been a staple for Indigenous Australians for centuries, connecting modern cuisine with traditional heritage.

Tips for Enjoying

Go Fresh: Opt for freshly caught barramundi whenever possible for the best taste and texture.

Try Different Styles: Sample it grilled, pan-fried, or served with an Asian-inspired sauce like miso or ginger-soy glaze.

Pair with Wine: A crisp white wine, like Sauvignon Blanc or Chardonnay, complements barramundi's flavor perfectly.

Season Simply: Minimal seasoning, such as salt, pepper, and lemon juice, highlights the natural taste.

Cook It Yourself: Purchase fresh barramundi from a local fish market and try grilling it with herbs and citrus at home.

5. Anzac Biscuits

Anzac biscuits are a traditional Australian and New Zealand treat, deeply tied to history and national identity. These chewy or crunchy cookies were originally made by families of soldiers in World War I and sent overseas due to their long shelf life and simple ingredients. The name "ANZAC" stands for the Australian and New Zealand Army Corps, and the biscuits remain a popular snack, often enjoyed with tea or coffee. Today, they symbolize remembrance and are commonly associated with Anzac Day on April 25th.

Main Ingredients

Anzac biscuits are made with pantry staples, including:

Rolled Oats: The key ingredient for texture and flavor.

Desiccated Coconut: Adds a subtle nutty taste.

Golden Syrup: Provides sweetness and a chewy texture.

Butter: Contributes richness and binds the ingredients.

Flour: Ensures structure.

Bicarbonate of Soda: Reacts with water and golden syrup to give the biscuits a light texture.

Notably, Anzac biscuits contain no eggs, which historically made them more durable for transport to soldiers.

Where to Try in Australia

You can find Anzac biscuits in various locations, including:

Local Bakeries: Freshly baked biscuits are available in bakeries across Australia.

Supermarkets: Packaged versions are widely sold in stores like Coles and Woolworths.

Cafes: Often served as a snack alongside coffee or tea.

Homemade: Many Australians bake them at home, particularly around Anzac Day, using traditional recipes.

Taste

Anzac biscuits are known for their satisfying balance of sweetness and nuttiness. The oats and coconut give them a hearty texture, while the golden syrup imparts a warm, caramel-like flavor. Depending on the recipe, they can range from soft and chewy to crisp and crunchy, catering to different preferences.

What Makes It Special?

Historical Significance: These biscuits are more than just a treat; they carry the legacy of soldiers and families from World War I.

Simplicity: Made from basic ingredients, Anzac biscuits are easy to prepare and enjoy.

Versatility: Whether you like them chewy or crunchy, they can be customized to suit your taste.

Cultural Symbolism: They're closely associated with Anzac Day, a significant national commemoration in Australia and New Zealand.

Tips for Enjoying

Serve with Tea or Coffee: Anzac biscuits pair wonderfully with a warm beverage.

Make Your Own: Try baking them at home to experience their historical charm and adjust the texture to your preference.

Add a Modern Twist: While traditional recipes are treasured, some enjoy adding extras like chocolate chips or dried fruit.

Store Properly: Keep them in an airtight container to maintain freshness.

Enjoy the Tradition: If visiting during Anzac Day, partake in the cultural significance by enjoying these biscuits while reflecting on their history.

Indigenous Food and Bush Tucker

Indigenous food, commonly known as "bush tucker," represents the traditional ingredients and cooking practices of Aboriginal Australians, honed over tens of thousands of years. Rooted in a deep understanding of the land, bush tucker features native plants, herbs, and animals sourced sustainably from Australia's diverse environments. Today, it offers tourists a unique opportunity to connect with the continent's ancient culture and biodiversity.

Bush tucker has gained popularity in modern cuisine, with chefs incorporating traditional ingredients into contemporary dishes. From kangaroo and emu to wattleseed and finger lime, experiencing Indigenous food is both a culinary and cultural journey that highlights the richness of Australia's heritage.

Common Bush Tucker Ingredients

Proteins

Kangaroo: Lean, gamey meat rich in protein and iron.

Emu: A low-fat, flavorful poultry option.

Crocodile: White meat with a texture similar to chicken or fish.

Goanna and Other Reptiles: Traditional meat sources in many Indigenous diets.

Fruits and Vegetables

Quandong: A tangy native peach.

Finger Lime: Often called "citrus caviar," with a zesty, burst-like texture.

Kakadu Plum: Rich in vitamin C, often used in sauces and desserts.

Bush Tomatoes: Small, tangy fruits used in chutneys and sauces.

Herbs and Spices

Wattleseed: A versatile seed with nutty and coffee-like flavors, often used in baking.

Lemon Myrtle: A fragrant herb with a citrusy flavor.

Pepperberry: A spicy alternative to black pepper.

Nuts and Seeds

Macadamia Nuts: Native to Australia and widely popular.

Bunya Nuts: A traditional nut harvested from Bunya pines.

Where to Try Indigenous Food in Australia

Cultural Tours: Join Indigenous-led tours in regions like Kakadu, the Kimberley, or Uluru, where guides showcase traditional bush foods in their natural habitats.

Restaurants: Fine dining establishments, such as those in Sydney or Melbourne, often feature bush tucker ingredients in gourmet dishes.

Bush Tucker Workshops: Learn to identify and prepare native ingredients in hands-on classes.

Local Markets: Farmers' markets and food festivals frequently offer bush tucker-inspired products.

Taste and Cooking Methods

Bush tucker flavors are diverse, ranging from sweet and tangy to smoky and earthy. Traditional cooking methods include roasting over open flames, baking in hot coals, and steaming in earth ovens. Modern chefs blend these flavors into contemporary dishes, such as kangaroo steaks with native spices or lemon myrtle-infused desserts, creating a fusion of ancient and modern tastes.

What Makes It Special?

Cultural Significance: Bush tucker connects visitors to the traditions, stories, and knowledge of Australia's First Nations people.

Sustainability: Indigenous food practices emphasize sustainable harvesting and respect for the environment.

Unique Flavors: Many bush tucker ingredients are found nowhere else in the world, offering an exclusive culinary experience.

Health Benefits: Native ingredients like wattleseed and Kakadu plum are rich in nutrients, making them both delicious and wholesome.

Tips for Enjoying Indigenous Food

Start with Guided Experiences: Indigenous-led tours or cultural centers provide the best introduction to bush tucker.

Experiment with Modern Dishes: Try dishes that incorporate bush foods into familiar recipes, such as desserts with wattleseed or cocktails with finger lime.

Respect the Culture: Engage with the stories and traditions behind the ingredients to gain a deeper appreciation of their significance.

Support Local Producers: Purchase bush tucker products from Indigenous businesses to support the community.

Be Adventurous: Don't shy away from trying unique ingredients like crocodile or pepperberry—it's part of the experience!

Top Restaurants and Dining Experiences

Top Restaurants

1. Quay (Sydney)

Cuisine: Modern Australian

Why Visit: With breathtaking views of the Sydney Opera House and Harbour Bridge, Quay is a must-visit for those seeking luxurious dining. Its meticulously crafted tasting menu features dishes like poached abalone and native-inspired desserts.

Ambiance: Elegant and contemporary.

2. Attica (Melbourne)

Cuisine: Indigenous and Modern Australian Fusion

Why Visit: Attica is celebrated for its incorporation of native ingredients such as kangaroo, finger lime, and wattleseed, presented in artful and imaginative ways. Chef Ben Shewry's creations often tell a story, making this a dining experience rather than just a meal.

Ambiance: Intimate and avant-garde.

3. Orana (Adelaide)

Cuisine: Contemporary Australian with Indigenous Influences

Why Visit: Chef Jock Zonfrillo's award-winning restaurant offers a deep dive into Indigenous flavors, showcasing ingredients like bunya nuts, green ants, and kangaroo tail in innovative dishes.

Ambiance: Chic yet understated, highlighting the food's authenticity.

4. Tasman Terrace (Hobart)

Cuisine: Seafood

Why Visit: Situated near the waterfront, this restaurant is perfect for indulging in Tasmania's freshest catches, such as oysters, abalone, and salmon. Pair with local wines for a complete experience.

Ambiance: Relaxed and scenic.

5. Nautilus Restaurant (Port Douglas)

Cuisine: Tropical and International Fusion

Why Visit: Dine under the stars in a lush rainforest setting. Nautilus specializes in tropical flavors with dishes like grilled barramundi and Moreton Bay bugs.

Ambiance: Romantic and serene.

Unique Dining Experiences

1. Sydney Tower Buffet (Sydney)

Experience: A revolving restaurant offering panoramic views of Sydney's skyline and a buffet featuring Australian classics like lamb roast and pavlova.

Perfect For: Tourists wanting a mix of views and variety.

2. Dinner Under the Stars at Uluru

Experience: Enjoy a magical outdoor dining experience at the "Sounds of Silence" event, with dishes featuring bush tucker like crocodile, emu, and quandong. Live didgeridoo performances enhance the cultural ambiance.

Perfect For: Those seeking cultural and natural immersion.

3. The Margaret River Food and Wine Trail (Western Australia)

Experience: A blend of gourmet dining and wine tasting at award-winning vineyards. Many wineries, such as Leeuwin Estate, offer exquisite meals paired with their finest wines.

Perfect For: Food and wine enthusiasts.

4. Barossa Valley Gourmet Experiences (South Australia)

Experience: Renowned for its world-class wines, Barossa Valley also offers fine dining experiences featuring local produce, cheeses, and charcuterie.

Perfect For: Couples and gastronomes.

5. Seafood Dining in Cairns

Experience: Freshly caught seafood served overlooking the Coral Sea. Try mud crabs, reef fish, or prawns paired with tropical cocktails.

Perfect For: Fans of alfresco dining and ocean views.

Tips for Enjoying Australian Dining

Make Reservations: Popular restaurants like Quay and Attica often require bookings weeks in advance.

Try Local Flavors: Sample native ingredients such as wattleseed, kangaroo, or macadamia nuts.

Pair with Australian Wine: Regions like Barossa Valley and Yarra Valley produce exceptional wines that elevate any meal.

Explore Street Food: Don't miss casual delights like meat pies, fish and chips, or Vegemite-inspired dishes in local markets.

Cultural Sensitivity: When dining on bush tucker, engage with the cultural stories behind the ingredients to enhance your experience.

Cafes and Street Food

Cafes in Australia

1. Melbourne: The Coffee Capital

Known as a global hub for café culture, Melbourne offers an array of artisanal coffee spots. Popular choices include:

Proud Mary: Renowned for its expertly brewed flat whites and single-origin coffee.

Axil Coffee Roasters: Famous for specialty roasts and brunch options like avocado toast.

2. Sydney: Beachside Cafés

Combine great coffee with stunning views. Notable spots include:

The Grounds of Alexandria: A café and garden with stunning decor and creative dishes.

Bondi Beach's Porch and Parlour: A relaxed spot offering coffee and healthy bowls.

3. Byron Bay: Laid-Back Vibes

Cafés in Byron Bay focus on organic and locally sourced ingredients. Check out:

Bayleaf Café: Known for its vibrant smoothie bowls and artisanal coffee.

Folk: A cozy, eco-friendly café with plant-based menu items.

4. Hobart: Tasmanian Delights

Small but mighty, Hobart's café scene offers locally roasted coffee and pastries:

Pilgrim Coffee: Beloved for its strong brews and hearty breakfasts.

Jackman & McRoss: Famous for freshly baked goods like meat pies and sourdough.

Street Food in Australia

1. Famous Street Food Dishes

Meat Pies: Found at bakeries, food stalls, and markets nationwide. A flaky pastry filled with meat and gravy, it's a quintessential Australian snack.

Sausage Sizzles: A classic Aussie BBQ sausage served in bread with onions and sauce, often sold at local markets and community events.

Fish and Chips: Best enjoyed by the beach, with fresh seafood and crispy golden fries.

Dim Sims: An Australian twist on Chinese dumplings, often deep-fried or steamed.

Chiko Rolls: A deep-fried snack inspired by egg rolls, filled with meat and veggies.

2. Popular Street Food Markets

Queen Victoria Market (Melbourne): A bustling spot offering everything from Greek souvlaki to freshly shucked oysters.

Sydney Fish Market: Perfect for seafood lovers, featuring sashimi, prawns, and lobster rolls.

Eumundi Markets (Sunshine Coast): Famous for international street food like Thai curries and vegan desserts.

Salamanca Market (Hobart): Offers artisanal products alongside street eats such as wood-fired pizzas and scallop pies.

Mindil Beach Sunset Market (Darwin): Known for tropical treats like mango smoothies and laksa.

Unique Street Food Experiences

1. Food Trucks

Sydney's Eat Art Truck: Known for its gourmet BBQ and creative street food.

Melbourne's Mr. Burger: Offers indulgent burgers, fries, and milkshakes.

2. Outback BBQ

Experience traditional Aussie BBQ in rural areas, with kangaroo, emu, and crocodile meat grilled to perfection.

3. Cultural Fusion

Australia's multicultural society has inspired a range of street food, from Vietnamese bánh mì sandwiches to Italian arancini balls and Turkish gozleme.

Regional Specialties

Regional Specialties by State and Territory

1. New South Wales (NSW)

Sydney Rock Oysters

Found along the NSW coastline, these oysters are prized for their creamy texture and distinct briny flavor.

Best enjoyed fresh or with a splash of lemon.

Pavlova

A meringue-based dessert topped with fresh fruit, often attributed to Australian heritage.

Try at local bakeries or fine dining restaurants.

2. Victoria (VIC)

Dim Sims

An Australian-Chinese fusion snack, these dumplings are larger than traditional versions and can be fried or steamed.

Found at food markets and takeaway shops.

Parma (Chicken Parmigiana)

A pub favorite, this dish features crumbed chicken topped with tomato sauce, cheese, and sometimes ham.

Served with chips and salad in pubs across Melbourne.

3. Queensland (QLD)

Barramundi

A flaky, mild-flavored fish popular in Queensland's coastal regions.

Often grilled, pan-fried, or baked with tropical herbs.

Mud Crabs

Caught fresh from Queensland's waters, these are best enjoyed in garlic butter or chili sauce.

4. South Australia (SA)

Coffin Bay Oysters

Famous for their premium quality and rich, creamy taste.

Served raw, grilled, or smoked in restaurants near Coffin Bay.

Frog Cakes

A quirky dessert featuring sponge cake covered in fondant, shaped like a frog's head.

Iconic to Adelaide and available at local bakeries.

5. Western Australia (WA)

Marron

A freshwater crayfish with sweet, delicate meat.

Often grilled or served with butter sauces in upscale restaurants.

Truffle Dishes

Western Australia is a significant producer of black truffles, featured in gourmet dishes like truffle pasta and risotto.

6. Tasmania (TAS)

Scallop Pies

A savory pie filled with scallops and a creamy curry sauce, unique to Tasmania.

Available at local bakeries and seafood festivals.

Tasmanian Salmon

Renowned for its quality and flavor, often served smoked or grilled.

Best paired with local wines.

7. Northern Territory (NT)

Kangaroo Tail Stew

A traditional Indigenous dish slow-cooked with native herbs and spices.

Served at cultural centers and bush tucker tours.

Crocodile Meat

White meat with a taste resembling chicken or fish.

Grilled crocodile burgers are a popular street food option.

8. Australian Capital Territory (ACT)

Canberra Truffles

Found in gourmet dishes across the region during the truffle season (June–August).

Try at truffle farms or local fine dining establishments.

Modern Australian Cuisine

Canberra features a blend of specialties due to its cosmopolitan dining scene.

Signature Ingredients by Region

Finger Limes (QLD): Known as "citrus caviar," often added to seafood dishes.

Pepperberries (TAS): Spicy and aromatic, used in sauces and marinades.

Kakadu Plum (NT): Rich in Vitamin C, featured in desserts and condiments.

Tips for Exploring Regional Specialties

Visit Local Markets: Sample authentic specialties like Coffin Bay oysters or scallop pies straight from the source.

Join Food Tours: Culinary tours in regions like Barossa Valley or Margaret River offer guided tastings and insights.

Attend Food Festivals: Events like the Taste of Tasmania or Melbourne Food and Wine Festival highlight regional cuisine.

Pair with Local Drinks: Match your meal with regional wines, craft beers, or artisanal spirits for a complete experience.

Ask the Locals: Recommendations from residents often lead to the best hidden gems.

Nightlife and Bars

Top Nightlife Destinations

1. Sydney

The Ivy

A multi-level entertainment hub featuring rooftop pools, dance floors, and chic lounges.

Opera Bar

Located by the Sydney Opera House, this bar combines stunning harbor views with a vibrant social atmosphere.

The Argyle

A historic sandstone venue in The Rocks offering a mix of DJs and themed nights.

2. Melbourne

Section 8

A trendy outdoor bar set in a shipping container, perfect for hipsters and casual vibes.

The Toff in Town

Known for live music and intimate booths, blending modern cocktails with entertainment.

Eau de Vie

A speakeasy-style bar offering theatrical cocktails and an old-world charm.

3. Brisbane

Cloudland

A luxurious venue with greenery-filled interiors, offering dance nights and fine dining.

The Gresham

A heritage-listed whiskey bar with a sophisticated yet relaxed atmosphere.

Riverbar and Kitchen

Perfect for drinks with views of the Brisbane River, serving creative cocktails and light bites.

4. Perth

Mechanics Institute

A rooftop bar known for its laid-back ambiance and excellent burger pairings.

Northbridge Nightlife

The heart of Perth's nightlife, offering pubs, clubs, and bars catering to various tastes.

Hula Bula Bar

A tiki bar serving exotic cocktails in a colorful, Polynesian-themed setting.

5. Adelaide

Hains & Co

Specializes in rum, gin, and whiskey, with a cozy, nautical-inspired interior.

Cry Baby

A retro bar with a rock 'n' roll vibe, offering jukebox tunes and classic drinks.

Peel Street

A hub for eclectic bars like Maybe Mae, a hidden cocktail bar with art deco flair.

6. Gold Coast

Elsewhere

A nightclub combining artsy decor with top-notch DJs and live acts.

Burleigh Pavilion

Overlooking the beach, this venue offers stylish drinks and breathtaking ocean views.

The Island Rooftop

A lively rooftop bar perfect for cocktails and dancing under the stars.

7. Tasmania (Hobart)

Preachers

A quirky bar housed in an old cottage, featuring a beer garden and food trucks.

The Glass House

A floating bar with panoramic views of Hobart's waterfront, serving fine wines and cocktails.

Gold Bar

Specializes in Tasmanian whiskies and locally crafted spirits.

8. Northern Territory (Darwin)

Monsoons

A lively spot for drinks, dance, and live entertainment.

Mindil Beach Sunset Bar

Best for enjoying cocktails while watching Darwin's iconic sunsets.

Deck Bar

A casual open-air venue offering an extensive drinks menu and a chill vibe.

Unique Nightlife Experiences

Rooftop Bars

Enjoy drinks with panoramic city views at places like Melbourne's Rooftop Bar or Sydney's Smoke at Barangaroo.

Live Music Venues

Discover Australia's thriving music scene at spots like Sydney's Enmore Theatre or Brisbane's The Triffid.

Craft Breweries and Distilleries

Tour venues like Little Creatures in Fremantle or Four Pillars Gin in Victoria for tastings.

Pub Crawls

Join organized pub tours to explore historic pubs in cities like Melbourne and Adelaide.

Casino Nights

Visit Crown Casino in Melbourne or The Star in Sydney for gaming, entertainment, and luxury dining.

What Makes Australia's Nightlife Special?

Diversity: Options range from upscale lounges to grungy dive bars, catering to all moods and styles.

Outdoor Venues: Rooftop bars, beach clubs, and beer gardens take advantage of Australia's warm climate.

Local Drinks: Many bars highlight Australian wines, craft beers, and spirits, offering a unique taste of the region.

Friendly Atmosphere: The laid-back vibe and welcoming locals make nights out enjoyable and stress-free.

Tips for Enjoying Nightlife in Australia

Check Entry Requirements: Some venues have dress codes or age restrictions.

Embrace Local Drinks: Try Australian wines, craft beers, and signature cocktails featuring native ingredients.

Plan Transportation: Use rideshares or public transport to ensure safe travels after a night out.

Explore Beyond Cities: Coastal towns and regional areas often feature unique and charming nightlife options.

Know the Peak Times: Most venues get lively after 9 PM, especially on weekends.

Chapter 10: Practical Information
Language and Communication

Official Language

English: The dominant language spoken across Australia is English. However, Australian English has its own distinct pronunciation, vocabulary, and slang, which can be fun to learn and understand.

Australian English and Slang

Australian Slang: Aussies are known for their colorful and relaxed slang, which may sound unfamiliar to visitors. Some common examples include:

G'day: Hello

Arvo: Afternoon

Mate: Friend or buddy

No worries: It's okay, or don't worry about it

Bogan: A term used for a person who is perceived as unsophisticated, often used humorously.

Thongs: Flip-flops (not underwear!)

Barbie: Barbecue

Footy: Australian Rules Football (or rugby, depending on the region)

Pronunciation: Aussies tend to shorten words and speak with a distinctive accent. For example, "fish and chips" might sound like "fish 'n' chips," and "afternoon" becomes "arvo."

Communication Tips

Polite and Friendly: Australians are generally friendly and informal, and they appreciate a laid-back, friendly approach in conversations. Saying "please" and "thank you" is always appreciated, though they tend to be more relaxed about formality than in some other cultures.

Small Talk: Australians enjoy chatting about sports, weather, and local happenings. Don't be surprised if a friendly stranger strikes up a conversation, especially in rural areas or at social gatherings.

Personal Space: Australians typically respect personal space and are not overly touchy, but a handshake is a common greeting. In some regions, a hug or cheek kiss among friends is also common.

Indigenous Languages

Indigenous Languages: Australia has a rich cultural heritage with more than 250 distinct Indigenous languages, though many are no longer widely spoken. While English is the dominant language, some communities may still use traditional languages. Certain Aboriginal and Torres Strait Islander words have become part of everyday language, such as "kangaroo," "boomerang," and "quokka."

Cultural Sensitivity: When communicating with Indigenous Australians, it's important to be respectful and mindful of cultural differences. Some communities may have strong language ties, and learning about their history and customs can deepen your understanding of the country's diverse culture.

Sign Language

Auslan (Australian Sign Language): Auslan is the official sign language used by the Australian Deaf community. It is recognized and used widely, especially in education, government, and public services.

Translation and Language Resources

Language Apps and Translators: While English is the primary language, if you're traveling to remote areas where an Indigenous language is spoken, you may want to download translation apps or carry a phrasebook. Language apps like Google Translate can also be helpful for signs or words in non-English languages.

Language in Tourism: Most signs, public information, and tourist materials are provided in English. However, in larger cities and tourist areas, you might also encounter other languages spoken by local residents from multicultural communities, including Mandarin, Italian, and Arabic.

Communication Etiquette

Tipping: Tipping is not mandatory in Australia, and service charges are usually included in bills. However, if you receive exceptional service, a tip of 5-10% is appreciated.

Phone and Internet: Australians use mobile phones extensively, and it's easy to stay connected with good coverage in most areas. Public phones are available in major cities but are less common in rural areas. Internet cafes are still found in cities, but most visitors use mobile devices for Wi-Fi.

Currency and Tipping

Currency: Australian Dollar (AUD)

Coins: Australia's coins come in denominations of 5 cents, 10 cents, 20 cents, 50 cents, $1, and $2.

Banknotes: Australian banknotes are colorful and made from polymer, making them durable and water-resistant. The denominations are $5, $10, $20, $50, and $100.

Currency Exchange:

ATMs and Banks: ATMs are widely available throughout Australia, and you can withdraw Australian dollars using international credit or debit cards. Currency exchange services are also available at airports, banks, and exchange offices.

Credit Cards and Payments: Credit cards (Visa, MasterCard, American Express) are widely accepted in most establishments, including restaurants, shops, and hotels. Contactless payments (using cards or mobile apps like Apple Pay or Google Pay) are also common and convenient.

Tipping in Australia

Tipping is not a major part of Australian culture, but it is appreciated for exceptional service. In general, service workers do not rely on tips for their income, as wages in Australia tend to be higher than in many other countries where tipping is customary.

When to Tip:

Restaurants: While tipping is not mandatory, it's customary to leave a tip of around 5-10% if you're satisfied with the service. In casual dining or fast food settings, tipping is not expected, but rounding up the bill is common for small amounts.

Cafes and Bars: Tipping is not typically expected in cafes or bars, but leaving small change or rounding up your bill is a nice gesture if the service was excellent.

Taxis and Rideshares: Taxi drivers may appreciate a small tip, usually rounding up to the nearest dollar. For rideshare services like Uber, tipping is not required, but some passengers choose to leave a tip if the driver was exceptionally helpful or friendly.

Hotel Staff: While tipping hotel staff is not common practice, it can be appreciated for services like housekeeping, bellhops, or concierge assistance. A tip of $1-$2 per night for housekeeping or $5 for bellhops is a reasonable amount.

Tour Guides: If you've enjoyed a guided tour, leaving a tip of around 10-15% of the tour price is appreciated but not obligatory.

Other Services: For services like spa treatments, hairdressers, or other personal services, tips are appreciated, usually around 10% if you feel the service was above expectations.

No Service Charge

Unlike in some countries, Australians do not automatically add a service charge to bills, so tipping is left to the discretion of the customer. However, you may find some restaurants in tourist areas that add a surcharge of 10-15% on public holidays or for large groups.

Round-Up Custom

In many cafes, bars, and smaller shops, it's common to simply round up the bill to the nearest dollar or leave the change. This is seen as a casual and easy way to leave a tip without going overboard.

Key Points to Remember

Tipping is optional and not expected in Australia, but it is appreciated for good service.

Credit cards are widely accepted, and ATMs are easily accessible for withdrawing cash if you prefer to tip in cash.

For most services, rounding up or leaving a small percentage (5-10%) is considered a generous and polite gesture.

Emergency Numbers and Healthcare

Emergency Numbers

In case of an emergency, it's important to know the relevant contact numbers:

Emergency Services (Police, Fire, Ambulance): 000

This is the primary emergency number in Australia for any urgent situations, including accidents, medical emergencies, or fires.

Dial 000 for immediate assistance, and the operator will direct you to the appropriate service (police, fire, ambulance).

Police (Non-Emergency): 131 444

For non-urgent police matters, such as reporting a crime that is no longer in progress, you can contact this number.

Poisons Information: 13 11 26

If you are concerned about poisoning or need urgent advice regarding substances, contact this helpline for assistance.

State-based Emergency Numbers: Some regions may have additional numbers for local services, but 000 is the national emergency number used across the country.

Healthcare System in Australia

Australia has a highly developed healthcare system, and healthcare services are generally of excellent quality. Visitors can access medical treatment at various levels, from general practitioners to emergency services, though it's important to understand the costs and coverage involved.

Medicare:

Medicare is Australia's publicly funded health system, which provides access to a wide range of medical services at little or no cost for Australian residents. Unfortunately, Medicare generally does not cover travelers unless they are from countries with reciprocal health care agreements with Australia (such as the UK, New Zealand, and some other countries).

Reciprocal Health Care Agreements: If you are from a country with an agreement, you may be eligible for subsidized healthcare services during your stay. However, this typically covers only necessary treatment (not elective or private services).

Private Health Insurance:

If you're not covered by Medicare, it's highly recommended that you purchase travel health insurance before visiting Australia. This can help cover the cost of emergency medical treatment, hospital stays, or prescriptions. Many insurers also offer coverage for medical evacuation and repatriation if needed.

Travel Insurance: Make sure your travel insurance includes health coverage, as private healthcare can be expensive for tourists without it.

General Healthcare Services:

GPs (General Practitioners): If you need to see a doctor during your trip, you can visit a GP (general practitioner). Consultations are usually available by appointment, and you may be required to pay upfront and claim reimbursement if you're covered by insurance.

Pharmacies: Pharmacies are readily available across Australia and can help with minor illnesses, medications, and over-the-counter remedies. Pharmacists can also offer advice on basic healthcare.

Hospitals and Clinics: For more serious health issues, Australia has a wide network of public and private hospitals offering comprehensive services. Public hospitals provide emergency treatment, but there may be costs associated with non-residents.

Healthcare Costs for Visitors

Healthcare costs for non-residents can vary. While emergency treatment at public hospitals is available to all, visitors will typically need to pay for any care they receive, unless they have travel health insurance or are from a country with a reciprocal healthcare agreement.

Emergency Care: If you need emergency medical treatment, you'll be treated at a hospital but may be billed for the service. The cost of emergency care can vary significantly, depending on the nature of the treatment and the hospital.

Private Healthcare: Private medical services, including visits to specialists or elective surgery, can be quite expensive without insurance coverage.

Pharmacies and Prescriptions

Pharmacies are widely available in cities, towns, and even more remote areas, and they offer a range of products, from over-the-counter medications to health advice.

Prescription Medication: If you require prescription medication while in Australia, you will need a valid prescription from a licensed doctor. In many cases, international prescriptions may not be accepted, so it's a good idea to bring sufficient medication with you or see a local doctor if needed.

Vaccinations: It's advisable to check with your healthcare provider before traveling to Australia to ensure that your vaccinations are up to date. While no specific vaccinations are required for entry into Australia, certain vaccines (e.g., tetanus, hepatitis A/B, and influenza) are recommended depending on your travel plans.

Travel Health Tips

Stay Hydrated and Protect Against the Sun: Australia's hot climate, especially in the summer months, can lead to dehydration and sunburn. Always carry water and use sunscreen (SPF 30 or higher), especially when spending time outdoors or on the beach.

Stay Safe in Wildlife Areas: While exploring Australia's natural landscapes, remember to take precautions when dealing with wildlife. Some animals, such as snakes and jellyfish, can be dangerous. Always follow safety guidelines in national parks and nature reserves.

Language Barrier in Healthcare

English is the primary language used in medical settings in Australia. However, translation services are available at hospitals and clinics if required. If you don't speak English fluently, consider having a translation app or a travel companion who speaks English to assist you.

Internet and SIM Cards

Internet Access

Wi-Fi Availability:

Wi-Fi is widely available throughout Australia, especially in cities and popular tourist areas. Most hotels, cafes, restaurants, and shopping centers offer free or paid Wi-Fi. However, the quality and speed can vary, so it's a good idea to check with the venue about their Wi-Fi availability and any usage limits.

Public Wi-Fi:

Many public spaces, such as airports, libraries, and some parks, offer free public Wi-Fi. While convenient, be cautious when using public networks, as they may not be secure. Using a VPN (Virtual Private Network) for added security is recommended when accessing sensitive information over public Wi-Fi.

Internet Cafes:
If you're looking for a more stable internet connection or need to print documents, internet cafes are still present in larger cities and some tourist areas. They offer pay-per-use services for internet browsing, printing, and even scanning.

SIM Cards and Mobile Phones

If you plan to use your phone for calls, texts, or data during your trip, you'll need a local SIM card. Australian mobile networks are reliable, and several options are available for short-term visitors.

Major Mobile Providers: Australia's major mobile providers are:

Telstra: Known for having the best coverage, especially in remote areas.

Optus: Offers good coverage in cities and urban areas.

Vodafone: Provides strong coverage in most areas, with competitive pricing.

Buying a SIM Card:

You can purchase a SIM card at major airports, shopping centers, or mobile phone stores. To buy a local SIM, you'll need to show your passport for identification. SIM cards are available with different data packages and call options, catering to tourists and short-term visitors.

Prepaid SIM Plans:

Prepaid SIM cards are the most convenient for tourists. These plans typically include data, texts, and calls, with various options based on your needs. Most prepaid plans are flexible, with no long-term commitment. Prices vary, but a standard plan might offer:

Data: Ranges from 1GB to 30GB or more, depending on the plan.

Calls and Texts: Local calls and texts are often included in the plan, with some options for international calls or texts.

Validity: Plans generally last 30 days, after which you can top up or switch to a new plan.

Where to Buy:

You can purchase SIM cards at the airport upon arrival, at mobile phone stores, supermarkets, or even convenience stores. You'll find SIM cards in tourist-focused areas as well as larger shopping malls.

Roaming with Your Own SIM:

If you prefer to use your home country's SIM card, check with your provider about international roaming options before your trip. However, roaming charges can be expensive, and coverage may be limited in remote areas, so switching to an Australian SIM is often a more cost-effective option.

Data Usage and Internet Speed

Australia's internet speeds are generally fast in urban areas, with 4G and 5G services widely available. In more remote areas, mobile data coverage may be limited, so make sure your provider offers good coverage in the areas you'll be visiting. If you plan to use mobile data extensively, consider purchasing a larger data plan to avoid extra charges.

Mobile Hotspots

If you don't want to use a local SIM card, another option is renting a mobile hotspot (also known as a pocket Wi-Fi device). These devices can be rented at major airports or through online services before you travel. They allow you to stay connected without swapping SIM cards, though they come with daily rental fees and data limits.

International SIM Cards and eSIMs

For a more hassle-free option, you can also opt for an international SIM card or eSIM, which allows you to use mobile data and make calls in multiple countries, including Australia. Many companies offer global SIM cards, and eSIMs are an excellent choice if your phone supports them.

Useful Tips:

Check Compatibility: Ensure your phone is unlocked before arriving in Australia so you can use a local SIM card. Most modern smartphones are compatible with Australian networks, but it's always best to check.

Top-Up Options: You can easily top up your prepaid SIM card online, through mobile apps, or by visiting a local retailer. Some providers also offer automatic top-up options.

Free Apps: Consider using messaging apps like WhatsApp, Viber, or Facebook Messenger to stay connected via Wi-Fi, as these services use data and don't require traditional phone plans.

Time Zones and Weather

Time Zones

Australia spans multiple time zones due to its large geographical size. There are **three primary time zones**, with some regions observing **Daylight Saving Time (DST)** during the warmer months.

Australian Western Standard Time (AWST) - UTC +08:00

This time zone applies to **Western Australia**, including cities like Perth.

No Daylight Saving Time is observed here.

Australian Central Standard Time (ACST) - UTC +09:30

This zone covers **South Australia, Northern Territory,** and **Broken Hill** in **New South Wales**.

Daylight Saving Time is observed in South Australia (UTC +10:30) from **October to April**.

Australian Eastern Standard Time (AEST) - UTC +10:00

This applies to **Queensland, New South Wales** (excluding Broken Hill), **Victoria, Tasmania,** and the **Australian Capital Territory**.

Daylight Saving Time is observed in New South Wales, Victoria, Tasmania, and the Australian Capital Territory (UTC +11:00) from **October to April**.

When planning your travel and activities, keep these time differences in mind, especially if you are crossing state borders. For example, flights between Sydney (AEST) and Perth (AWST) can involve a **two-hour time difference**.

Weather

Australia's climate is diverse, with different regions experiencing varying weather patterns. The weather largely depends on the time of year and the region you're in. Here's an overview of what to expect:

Summer (December to February):

Temperature: Temperatures range from 25°C (77°F) in southern cities like Melbourne to over 40°C (104°F) in the central and northern regions.

Weather: This is Australia's peak travel season, with warm weather and lots of outdoor activities. In coastal cities like Sydney and Brisbane, summer is great for beachgoers. However, inland areas, such as the Outback, can become extremely hot, with heatwaves possible.

Best for: Visiting the beach, exploring cities, and enjoying festivals.

Autumn (March to May):

Temperature: Temperatures start to cool, ranging between 18°C (64°F) and 25°C (77°F) in southern regions, while the northern regions remain mild.

Weather: This is one of the most pleasant times to visit, with moderate temperatures and fewer crowds. Autumn is great for outdoor activities, such as hiking and exploring wine regions.

Best for: Outdoor adventures and enjoying the countryside.

Winter (June to August):

Temperature: Winter temperatures range from 5°C (41°F) in the southern parts to 20°C (68°F) in the tropical north.

Weather: Southern areas like Melbourne, Canberra, and Tasmania experience cooler, even frosty, temperatures with the possibility of snow in mountainous regions. In contrast, the northern regions, like Queensland and the Top End, have mild to warm temperatures and are ideal for a winter getaway.

Best for: Skiing in the mountains and escaping to warmer northern regions.

Spring (September to November):

Temperature: Spring brings warming temperatures from 15°C (59°F) to 26°C (79°F).

Weather: The weather is mild and ideal for outdoor activities like hiking, road trips, and exploring wildlife. Spring is a great time for wildflower festivals, especially in the southwest of Western Australia.

Best for: Visiting national parks, beaches, and wildlife watching.

Regional Variations

Northern Australia (Queensland, Northern Territory, and parts of Western Australia):

This region has a tropical climate with hot, humid summers and mild, dry winters. The wet season (November to April) brings heavy rains, particularly in tropical areas like Cairns and Darwin.

Southern Australia (Victoria, Tasmania, South Australia):

The southern states have a temperate climate, with cooler winters and milder summers. Tasmania can experience a lot of rainfall and cooler temperatures year-round.

Eastern Australia (New South Wales):

The eastern coast enjoys a mix of subtropical and temperate climates. Sydney, for example, experiences warm summers and mild winters, perfect for year-round beach activities.

Outback and Central Australia (Northern Territory, South Australia, and Western Australia):

The Outback has a hot desert climate, with scorching summers and cooler winters. Temperatures can fluctuate dramatically between day and night, especially in regions like Uluru (Ayers Rock) and Alice Springs.

What to Pack

Summer (December to February): Light clothing, sunscreen, sunglasses, a hat, and swimwear. If traveling inland, pack light layers, but also bring warmer clothing for cooler evenings.

Autumn and Spring (March to May & September to November): Pack light layers, a waterproof jacket, comfortable shoes, and sunscreen. The weather can be unpredictable, especially in the mountains or during sudden rain showers.

Winter (June to August): If heading to southern regions, pack a warm jacket, thermal layers, and gloves, especially if you're visiting the mountains or Tasmania.

Electrical Plugs and Voltage

Plug Type

Australia uses **Type I** electrical plugs, which have **three flat pins** arranged in a **V shape**. This type of plug is unique to Australia and a few other countries, such as New Zealand and Papua New Guinea.

Plug shape: Three flat pins in a triangular formation (two vertical and one horizontal).

Voltage: 230V

Frequency: 50Hz

Voltage and Frequency

Voltage: Australia operates on a **230V** electrical system. If your devices are not compatible with 230V, you will need a **voltage converter** to avoid damaging your electronics.

Frequency: The frequency is **50Hz**, which is common in most parts of the world.

Device Compatibility

Before using your devices in Australia, check whether they are compatible with **230V** and **50Hz**. Most modern electronic devices, such as laptops, phones, and cameras, are built with **dual voltage** (100-240V) and will work fine in Australia with just a plug adapter.

However, if your devices only support **110V** (common in countries like the United States), you will need a **voltage converter** or transformer in addition to a plug adapter.

Plug Adapters

If your plug type is different from Type I, you'll need a **plug adapter** to connect your devices to Australian power outlets. These adapters are widely available at travel stores, airports, and online retailers.

Safety Tips

Avoid using devices without a voltage converter if they are not compatible with 230V to prevent electrical damage.

Use a surge protector if you're plugging sensitive devices into Australian outlets, especially in areas where power fluctuations may occur.

Chapter 11: Sustainable Travel in Australia
Eco-Friendly Travel Practices

1. Minimize Plastic Waste

Avoid Single-Use Plastics: Australia's beaches and wildlife are often threatened by plastic pollution. Bring reusable items such as water bottles, shopping bags, and food containers.

Use Refillable Bottles: Many public spaces and attractions in Australia offer water refill stations. Carrying your own refillable water bottle reduces plastic waste.

2. Respect Wildlife and Habitats

Observe from a Distance: Australia's wildlife is diverse and fascinating, but it's crucial to respect their space. Avoid touching, feeding, or disturbing animals. Use binoculars or cameras for closer views without disturbing their natural behaviors.

Stick to Designated Trails: When hiking, camping, or exploring natural areas, always stay on marked paths to avoid damaging fragile ecosystems, especially in national parks and protected areas.

3. Choose Eco-Friendly Accommodation

Stay at Sustainable Lodgings: Look for accommodations that have eco-certifications, such as Green Star, EarthCheck, or the Eco Certification Program, which indicate sustainable practices like water and energy conservation, waste reduction, and local sourcing.

Support Eco-Friendly Hotels: Many hotels are adopting sustainable practices such as solar power, water-saving technologies, and waste recycling. Opt for those that prioritize sustainability.

4. Opt for Sustainable Transportation

Public Transport: Use trains, trams, and buses to reduce your carbon footprint. Many Australian cities have excellent public transport systems that are both convenient and eco-friendly.

Bike Rentals: Consider renting a bike to explore urban areas or nature reserves. Cycling reduces emissions and provides an opportunity to experience destinations in a more intimate and eco-conscious way.

Electric Vehicles: If renting a car, choose an **electric vehicle (EV)** or hybrid to lower your carbon impact. Several cities, including Melbourne and Sydney, have EV charging stations.

5. Conserve Water

Be Mindful of Water Usage: Australia is a relatively dry country with areas facing water scarcity. Use water sparingly, especially in remote or rural areas. Turn off taps when not In use, take shorter showers, and avoid wasting water.

Support Water-Conscious Businesses: Choose restaurants, accommodations, and tour operators who implement water-saving measures, like low-flow toilets and rainwater harvesting.

6. Support Local and Sustainable Businesses

Eat Locally Sourced Food: Opt for restaurants that offer organic, locally sourced, and seasonal food. This supports local farmers and reduces the carbon footprint of imported goods.

Buy Local Products: Support artisans, farmers, and local craftspeople by purchasing handmade and locally produced items, which helps reduce the environmental impact of mass-produced goods.

7. Offset Carbon Emissions

Carbon Offset Programs: Consider offsetting the carbon emissions of your flight through environmental organizations that plant trees or fund renewable energy projects. Many airlines also offer carbon offset options during booking.

8. Leave No Trace

Pack Out What You Pack In: Leave no trace by cleaning up after yourself. Whether you're at a beach, hiking trail, or a national park, always dispose of your trash properly or take it with you if no facilities are available.

Avoid Polluting Natural Areas: Stay clear of littering in national parks, beaches, and other pristine natural areas. Even small items like cigarette butts or plastic wrappers can have a lasting negative impact on ecosystems.

Responsible Tourism Guidelines

1. Respect Local Culture and Traditions

Learn About Indigenous Cultures: Australia is home to a rich Indigenous history that spans over 65,000 years. Before visiting Indigenous communities or cultural sites, take the time to learn about their traditions, languages, and histories. Participate in tours led by local Indigenous guides to gain deeper insights into their culture and knowledge.

Respect Sacred Sites: Some areas, like **Uluru** and parts of **Kakadu National Park**, hold deep cultural and spiritual significance for Indigenous Australians. Always respect local customs, follow guidelines, and avoid climbing or touching sacred landmarks when requested.

2. Support Local Communities

Stay in Locally-Owned Accommodation: Opt for locally-run hotels, guesthouses, and hostels instead of large international chains. This helps funnel money into the local economy and supports small businesses.

Buy Local: Purchase locally made products, crafts, and food, which supports artisans, farmers, and small producers. This reduces the environmental impact of shipping goods across long distances and ensures that profits stay within the community.

Respect Local Practices and Customs: Be mindful of social norms and practices. What may seem acceptable in your home country might not be in Australia, especially in rural or Indigenous areas. Always be respectful of the people and their way of life.

3. Be Mindful of Environmental Impact

Minimize Waste: Australia's ecosystems, including its oceans, beaches, and national parks, are vulnerable to pollution. Reduce waste by bringing reusable water bottles, bags, and containers. Avoid single-use plastics and dispose of your trash properly.

Conserve Water and Energy: Given the country's dry climate, it's important to be conscious of water usage. Don't leave taps running, take shorter showers, and use water-efficient facilities when available. Also, reduce energy consumption by turning off lights and appliances when not in use.

4. Choose Sustainable Transportation

Public Transport: Using public transport is one of the easiest ways to reduce your carbon footprint. Australia's major cities like Sydney, Melbourne, and Brisbane offer extensive public transport systems that are eco-friendly and convenient.

Walk or Cycle: For short distances, walking or cycling not only helps reduce emissions but also gives you a chance to immerse yourself in the local surroundings. Many cities and regional areas offer bike rental services for tourists.

Carbon Offset: If you're flying to Australia, consider offsetting your carbon emissions through environmental organizations. Many airlines offer carbon offset programs that fund projects like renewable energy or tree planting.

5. Protect Wildlife and Natural Resources

Observe, Don't Disturb: Australia's wildlife is unique and often fragile. Always observe animals from a distance and never feed them, as human food can harm wildlife. Be mindful of your presence to avoid disturbing their natural behaviors.

Follow Leave No Trace Principles: Whether you're hiking in the outback or visiting a beach, follow the principles of **Leave No Trace**. This means leaving the environment as you found it—no littering, disturbing wildlife, or damaging plant life.

Conserve Marine Life: Australia is home to the Great Barrier Reef, one of the world's most biodiverse ecosystems. While snorkeling or diving, avoid touching coral or marine life, and follow guidelines to minimize your impact on the reef.

6. Respect Animal Welfare

Avoid Activities that Exploit Animals: Be cautious of tours or attractions that involve animal exploitation, such as those that encourage interactions with wild animals for entertainment purposes. Choose ethical animal experiences, such as wildlife sanctuaries and eco-tours that focus on conservation and education.

Adopt Ethical Wildlife Viewing Practices: Only participate in wildlife tours that prioritize the well-being of the animals. Respect the guidelines set by tour operators and avoid activities that could harm or stress animals, such as riding elephants or taking photos with captive wildlife.

7. Support Eco-Friendly Tour Operators

Choose Sustainable Tours: Select tour operators that prioritize sustainability. Look for companies that minimize their environmental impact, use local guides, and educate travelers on conservation and cultural preservation. These operators often hold eco-certifications that ensure their commitment to responsible practices.

Consider Eco-Tourism: Australia offers a wide variety of eco-tourism experiences, such as guided bushwalks, wildlife safaris, and eco-lodges. These tours are designed to educate tourists about the natural world while minimizing environmental harm.

8. Be Aware of Local Issues

Stay Informed: Stay up-to-date with local environmental and social issues, such as wildlife conservation efforts, water conservation, and land management. Being aware of these challenges helps you make informed decisions about your travel choices.

Support Conservation Efforts: Many organizations in Australia focus on wildlife conservation, environmental protection, and Indigenous rights. Consider donating to or volunteering with these organizations during your trip.

Wildlife Protection

1. Observe Wildlife from a Distance

Respect Natural Behaviors: When viewing wildlife, always maintain a safe distance. Approaching or disturbing animals can cause stress and alter their natural behaviors, which can negatively impact their health and well-being.

Use Binoculars or Cameras: For a closer view, use binoculars or a camera with a zoom lens instead of approaching animals directly. This helps protect both you and the wildlife.

2. Avoid Feeding Wild Animals

Feeding Animals is Harmful: While it may seem tempting to feed wild animals, it can disrupt their natural diet and behavior. Feeding them human food can cause health problems, alter their foraging habits, and make them more reliant on humans for food.

Support Natural Feeding Habits: Let wildlife forage and hunt for food as they normally would. This helps maintain a balanced ecosystem and ensures that animals are healthy and self-sufficient.

3. Choose Ethical Wildlife Experiences

Support Conservation-Oriented Attractions: Look for wildlife sanctuaries, national parks, and conservation-focused tours that prioritize the protection and rehabilitation of animals. These organizations work to educate the public and preserve habitats, often offering immersive experiences with animals in their natural environments.

Avoid Wildlife Exploitation: Be cautious of attractions that exploit animals for entertainment, such as places where you can have close-up photos with captive animals or participate in activities that cause harm to animals. Choose ethical wildlife experiences that emphasize respect for animals and their habitats.

4. Protect Marine Life

Responsible Snorkeling and Diving: When visiting the Great Barrier Reef or other marine environments, follow all guidelines to protect coral reefs and marine species. Avoid touching coral or marine animals, as this can harm fragile ecosystems and disrupt marine life.

Avoid Plastic Pollution: Plastic pollution is a significant threat to marine life. Bring reusable bottles, bags, and containers to reduce your waste, and make sure you dispose of your trash properly, especially when at the beach or in natural environments.

5. Participate in Conservation Efforts

Support Wildlife Protection Charities: There are numerous organizations dedicated to protecting Australia's wildlife, such as the Australian Conservation Foundation, Wildlife Victoria, and the Australian Koala Foundation. Consider donating to or volunteering with these groups to directly contribute to conservation efforts.

Volunteer on Conservation Projects: Some tour operators offer volunteer programs where you can help protect wildlife and their habitats. These programs may involve tasks like wildlife monitoring, habitat restoration, and raising awareness about conservation issues.

6. Follow Local Guidelines and Regulations

Abide by Local Laws: Australia has strict laws regarding the protection of wildlife and their habitats. Be sure to follow all regulations when visiting parks, reserves, and wildlife areas. These rules are designed to protect both visitors and wildlife.

Respect Protected Areas: Many of Australia's wildlife habitats are protected by national and state laws. Stick to marked trails, stay within designated viewing areas, and respect access restrictions in these areas to prevent damage to delicate ecosystems.

7. Reduce Your Carbon Footprint

Support Sustainable Tourism: Opt for eco-friendly accommodations, transportation, and tours that aim to reduce environmental impact. Reducing your carbon footprint helps combat climate change, which is one of the biggest threats to Australia's wildlife.

Offset Your Travel Emissions: If you are flying to Australia, consider participating in carbon offset programs that invest in projects to reduce greenhouse gas emissions, such as reforestation or renewable energy initiatives.

Sustainable Accommodations and Eco-Tours

Sustainable Accommodations

When choosing where to stay, look for accommodations that are committed to sustainability through practices like energy conservation, waste reduction, and water management. Here are some examples of sustainable accommodations in Australia:

1. Eco-Lodges and Retreats

Off-the-Grid Lodging: Eco-lodges and retreats are designed to have minimal impact on the environment, often utilizing renewable energy sources such as solar or wind power. These accommodations typically emphasize conservation, offer locally sourced food, and use eco-friendly materials in their construction.

Examples:

Gwinganna Lifestyle Retreat in Queensland offers eco-conscious practices, organic food, and a focus on wellness and sustainability.

Ecocamp in Tasmania features eco-friendly cabins and operates within a nature reserve, offering guests an immersive experience in the wilderness.

2. Sustainable Hotels and Resorts

Green Certifications: Many hotels in Australia are now certified with **Green Star** or **EarthCheck** ratings, which indicate that they follow environmentally responsible practices, such as energy-efficient lighting, water-saving technologies, and waste reduction programs.

Examples:

Ovolo Hotels in Sydney and Melbourne are committed to sustainability, using energy-efficient systems, reducing waste, and promoting local produce in their restaurants.

The Crystalbrook Collection in Cairns features eco-luxury accommodations with a focus on reducing its carbon footprint and supporting sustainable tourism practices.

3. Farm Stays and Eco-Friendly Camping

Farm Stays: Staying on a working farm or eco-property offers an opportunity to connect with nature while supporting sustainable agricultural practices. Many of these accommodations focus on organic farming and eco-friendly initiatives.

Eco-Camping and Glamping: For those looking to experience the outdoors in comfort, glamping sites across Australia offer eco-friendly luxury tents and accommodations that blend nature with sustainable practices.

Eco-Tours in Australia

Eco-tours allow travelers to explore Australia's stunning landscapes while minimizing their environmental impact and supporting conservation efforts. Here are some eco-tour options:

1. Wildlife Tours

Sustainable Wildlife Experiences: Many eco-tour operators focus on wildlife conservation and offer responsible wildlife tours that allow you to observe animals in their natural habitats without disturbing them. These tours often promote awareness about local conservation efforts and educate visitors on how to protect vulnerable species.

Examples:

Wildlife Coast Cruises in Victoria offers eco-friendly tours where guests can spot whales, seals, and other marine life while learning about their natural environments and the need for protection.

Kangaroo Island Wildlife Tours in South Australia provides guided tours that focus on the island's unique wildlife and the importance of protecting its natural ecosystems.

2. Nature and Adventure Tours

Eco-Friendly Adventure Activities: From guided bushwalks and hikes to eco-friendly kayaking and cycling tours, adventure travel in Australia can be done sustainably. Many tour operators offer activities that prioritize safety and environmental responsibility.

Examples:

Daintree Eco Lodge & Spa in Queensland offers guided walks through the Daintree Rainforest, one of the world's oldest tropical rainforests, with a focus on conservation and environmental education.

Tasmanian Expeditions offers eco-conscious hiking and trekking tours through Tasmania's wild landscapes, including UNESCO World Heritage sites like the Cradle Mountain-Lake St Clair National Park.

3. Eco-Cruises and Sailing Tours

Sustainable Sailing: Exploring Australia's coastlines and islands on a sailing cruise is a great way to travel sustainably. Many sailing companies offer eco-tours that promote low-impact travel, such as small boat cruises, solar-powered yachts, and educational trips about marine conservation.

Examples:

Coral Expeditions offers eco-friendly cruises that focus on sustainability, low-impact travel, and support for marine conservation efforts around Australia's northern coastline and the Great Barrier Reef.

The Whitsundays Eco-Sailing company offers tours around the Whitsunday Islands with an emphasis on environmental protection and respect for marine life.

4. Indigenous Cultural and Nature Tours

Cultural Awareness and Conservation: Eco-tours often include opportunities to engage with Indigenous communities, where you can learn about their deep connection to the land and their efforts to protect natural resources. Many tours support Indigenous-led conservation projects, allowing you to experience Australia's cultural heritage while promoting sustainable tourism.

Examples:

Indigenous Walkabout Tours in Melbourne and Sydney offer guided tours that incorporate storytelling, local history, and Indigenous perspectives on environmental conservation.

Jarramali Rock Art Tours in Queensland combines cultural heritage and environmental awareness, offering visitors a chance to learn about Indigenous rock art and how it relates to the natural world.

Why Choose Sustainable Accommodations and Eco-Tours?

Minimize Environmental Impact: By choosing sustainable accommodations and eco-tours, you're directly contributing to the protection of Australia's unique natural environments. These practices reduce the ecological footprint of tourism and help preserve Australia's natural beauty for future generations.

Support Local Communities: Sustainable accommodations and eco-tours often prioritize local businesses, employing local guides and artisans and supporting local conservation projects. This ensures that the benefits of tourism stay within the community and contribute to its economic growth.

Enhance Your Experience: Sustainable travel experiences tend to be more immersive and educational, allowing you to learn about local ecosystems, wildlife, and Indigenous cultures while also connecting more deeply with your surroundings.

Chapter 12: Day Trips and Short Escapes
Blue Mountains from Sydney

Highlights of the Blue Mountains

The Blue Mountains region is a UNESCO World Heritage site known for its diverse wildlife, pristine wilderness, and dramatic rock formations. Some of the must-see sights include:

1. Three Sisters

This iconic rock formation at Echo Point in Katoomba is one of the most famous landmarks in the Blue Mountains. The Three Sisters are surrounded by breathtaking views of the Jamison Valley and are steeped in Indigenous legend. It's a perfect spot for photos and offers an easy walk with panoramic views.

2. Scenic World

For a unique experience, visit **Scenic World** in Katoomba, where you can ride the **Scenic Railway** (the world's steepest passenger railway) or the **Scenic Skyway**, which provides spectacular views over the valley, cliffs, and rainforest. The **Scenic Cableway** takes you down to the forest floor, offering a different perspective of the Blue Mountains.

3. Wentworth Falls

This stunning waterfall is a highlight for nature lovers. There are several walking tracks leading to different viewpoints, including the challenging **Wentworth Falls Track**, which offers spectacular views of the falls and the surrounding forest.

4. Leura Village

The charming town of **Leura** is known for its boutique shops, cafes, and gardens. Take a stroll down the main street, or visit **Everglades Gardens**, a heritage-listed garden with European-style landscaping and views over the mountains.

5. Grand Canyon Walk

For those who enjoy a more adventurous walk, the **Grand Canyon Walk** is a popular choice. It takes you deep into the lush canyon, where you'll pass through rainforest, cross streams, and encounter striking rock formations.

Things to Do in the Blue Mountains

1. Bushwalking and Hiking

The Blue Mountains are a paradise for hiking enthusiasts, with trails suitable for all levels. From leisurely walks to more challenging hikes, there's something for everyone. Popular trails include the **National Pass** (for stunning valley views) and the **Grand Canyon Walk** (a beautiful, forested trail).

2. Wildlife Spotting

The Blue Mountains are home to a range of unique wildlife, including kangaroos, wallabies, lyrebirds, and a variety of native plants. Look out for these creatures while walking through the bush or from one of the many scenic viewpoints.

3. Aboriginal Cultural Experiences

Discover the rich Aboriginal heritage of the region with guided tours or cultural experiences. Learn about the **Darug people**, the traditional custodians of the land, and hear stories about their connection to the Blue Mountains and its spiritual significance.

4. Photography

Whether you're a professional photographer or just love taking pictures, the Blue Mountains offer endless opportunities for stunning shots. The dramatic cliff faces, cascading waterfalls, and mist-covered valleys make for spectacular photographs, especially at sunrise and sunset.

How to Get There

The Blue Mountains are easily accessible from Sydney, just about 1.5 to 2 hours by car, making it a perfect day trip. If you prefer public transport, you can take a **train from Central Station in Sydney** to Katoomba, the main hub of the Blue Mountains. Trains run regularly, and the journey offers scenic views along the way.

When to Visit

The Blue Mountains are a year-round destination, each season offering something special:

Spring and Summer (September to February): Enjoy mild temperatures, perfect for bushwalking and outdoor activities. The region's gardens and wildflowers are in full bloom, creating a colorful landscape.

Autumn (March to May): The cooler weather and vibrant autumn foliage make this an ideal time to visit for those who enjoy a peaceful, scenic getaway.

Winter (June to August): Winter brings crisp, cool weather, and the chance to see the mountains dusted with snow, adding a magical touch to the region.

Tips for Visiting

Wear Comfortable Shoes: Many of the Blue Mountains' trails are rugged, so be sure to wear sturdy footwear suitable for hiking.

Pack Water and Snacks: Although there are cafes and restaurants in towns like Katoomba and Leura, it's a good idea to carry water and snacks for the hikes and remote areas.

Check the Weather: The weather can change quickly in the mountains, so bring layers and be prepared for rain, especially in winter and spring.

Great Barrier Reef from Cairns

Why Visit the Great Barrier Reef from Cairns?

Cairns is strategically located on the edge of the Great Barrier Reef, making it the ideal starting point for exploring this natural wonder. With its warm tropical climate, clear waters, and proximity to reef sites, Cairns offers an easy gateway for both beginners and seasoned divers to experience the reef in all its glory.

Highlights of the Great Barrier Reef

Reef Sites: Cairns is home to several reef locations easily accessible via day trips, including **Green Island**, **Fitzroy Island**, and the **Outer Reef**. These sites feature vibrant coral gardens, abundant marine life, and crystal-clear waters, offering fantastic opportunities for snorkeling, diving, and glass-bottom boat tours.

Marine Life: The Great Barrier Reef is one of the most biodiverse ecosystems in the world. Expect to encounter an incredible variety of marine life, including tropical fish, sea turtles, stingrays, and even majestic manta rays and sharks. Depending on the time of year, you may also spot migrating whales or even the elusive dugong.

Coral Gardens: The reef's coral gardens are a kaleidoscope of colors and formations. You'll see vibrant soft and hard corals, massive coral bommies, and undersea valleys teeming with life. Snorkelers and divers can explore these underwater landscapes at various depths, while non-swimmers can enjoy the views from the comfort of a glass-bottom boat.

Popular Reef Activities

Snorkeling

If you don't want to dive but still want to experience the beauty of the reef, snorkeling is an excellent option. Most reef tours from Cairns offer snorkeling opportunities at shallow, calm spots, perfect for beginners and families. The warm, clear water makes it easy to see the colorful coral and marine life just below the surface.

Scuba Diving

Cairns is one of the best places in Australia for scuba diving, with a wide range of dive operators offering trips to both the inner and outer reefs. The waters around the Great Barrier Reef are known for their excellent visibility, and divers of all levels can explore the reef's incredible underwater landscape. Experienced divers will appreciate the opportunity to dive at deeper sites, while beginners can take introductory courses to experience the reef with an instructor.

Glass-Bottom Boat Tours

For those who prefer to stay dry but still want to marvel at the underwater world, glass-bottom boat tours are a great way to view the reef without getting in the water. These tours provide an up-close view of the coral gardens and marine life through the boat's glass panels, making it accessible for everyone, including those with limited mobility or young children.

Helicopter Tours

For a bird's-eye view of the Great Barrier Reef, consider booking a **helicopter tour**. Flying over the reef gives you a unique perspective of its size and beauty, with the coral formations appearing as intricate patterns in the turquoise waters below. Some tours even fly over iconic sites like **Heart Reef**, a naturally occurring heart-shaped coral formation that's especially popular with couples and honeymooners.

How to Get to the Great Barrier Reef from Cairns

Cairns is the main gateway to the Great Barrier Reef, and getting to the reef is easy. Daily boat trips depart from Cairns, taking you to various reef locations. These boat tours typically last from 4 to 8 hours, depending on the destination, and include onboard facilities like lunch, snorkel gear, and wetsuits. You can choose from group tours or private charters, depending on your preferences and budget.

Additionally, if you're interested in exploring multiple sites, some tours offer the option to visit several reef locations in one day, allowing you to maximize your time on the water.

Best Time to Visit

The Great Barrier Reef can be visited year-round, but certain times of the year offer better experiences:

May to October: The dry season is considered the best time to visit, with calm seas, clear skies, and ideal water temperatures for snorkeling and diving.

November to April: This is the wet season, characterized by higher humidity and occasional storms. While the reef is still accessible, you may experience fewer sunny days and the waters can be a bit murkier. However, this is also when the reef is busiest with tourists, so booking in advance is advisable.

Tips for Visiting the Great Barrier Reef

Sun Protection: The tropical sun can be intense, so make sure to wear sunscreen, a hat, and protective clothing, especially when spending time on the water.

Stay Hydrated: The heat can be strong, so carry plenty of water with you, especially during boat tours or when snorkeling.

Check Weather Conditions: The weather can change quickly, especially in the wet season. Make sure to check weather reports before heading out on a boat trip.

Book in Advance: The Great Barrier Reef is a major tourist attraction, so it's best to book your reef trip in advance, particularly during the high season, to secure your spot.

Yarra Valley Wine Tour from Melbourne

Why Visit the Yarra Valley?

The Yarra Valley is one of Australia's oldest wine regions, renowned for its cool-climate wines, particularly **Pinot Noir**, **Chardonnay**, and **Shiraz**. It's a perfect day trip for wine lovers, foodies, and anyone looking to escape Melbourne's hustle and bustle. The region is not only famous for its wine but also for its stunning scenery, local produce, and excellent dining options.

Highlights of a Yarra Valley Wine Tour

Vineyards and Wineries: The Yarra Valley is home to over 80 wineries, many of which offer cellar door tastings. Whether you're a wine connoisseur or a casual drinker, you'll enjoy tasting some of the region's finest wines while soaking in breathtaking views of the vineyards. Many wineries offer guided tours, giving you an insight into the winemaking process from grape to glass.

Gourmet Dining: The Yarra Valley is a food lover's paradise, with a range of fine dining restaurants, casual eateries, and gourmet food shops. Enjoy meals made from fresh, locally sourced ingredients, perfectly paired with wines from the region. Whether you're having a long lunch at a winery restaurant or sampling artisanal cheeses, chocolates, and fresh produce at local markets, you're sure to be impressed by the food culture here.

Scenic Views and Nature: The Yarra Valley is not just about wine – it's also about the stunning scenery. As you tour the wineries, you'll pass through picturesque landscapes of rolling hills, lush forests, and winding rivers. For those who enjoy nature, the region also offers plenty of walking trails and opportunities to enjoy the outdoors.

Historic Sites: While wine is the main attraction, the Yarra Valley also has a rich history. Visit **Healesville**, a charming town in the heart of the valley, known for its historic buildings and vibrant arts scene. You can also explore the **Healesville Sanctuary**, an Australian wildlife park that focuses on native species conservation.

Top Wineries to Visit

Domaine Chandon: Famous for its sparkling wines, Domaine Chandon offers an elegant experience with breathtaking views. Enjoy a glass of bubbly while looking over the rolling hills of the valley.

Yering Station: Known as one of the oldest wineries in the region, Yering Station is a must-visit for its elegant cellar door and award-winning wines. The vineyard is also home to a contemporary restaurant with delicious food and wine pairings.

Chandon Australia: If you're a fan of sparkling wines, Chandon is the place to go. This winery offers tours, tastings, and sparkling wine-focused experiences with views over the beautiful Yarra Valley.

Coldstream Hills: Renowned for its cool-climate wines, particularly Pinot Noir and Chardonnay, Coldstream Hills is a boutique winery offering tastings and a cozy atmosphere to enjoy the best of Yarra Valley wines.

Popular Tour Activities

Wine Tastings: At most wineries, you'll have the opportunity to sample a selection of wines from the region. Many cellar doors offer structured tastings led by experts who can teach you about the unique characteristics of the Yarra Valley terroir.

Food and Wine Pairings: Many wineries feature gourmet restaurants where you can enjoy food and wine pairings. Try local cheeses, meats, and fresh produce alongside handpicked wines for a complete culinary experience.

Wine and Chocolate Pairing: A special treat for those with a sweet tooth, some wineries in the region offer wine and chocolate tasting experiences. Savor handcrafted chocolates paired with premium wines for a delightful indulgence.

Hot Air Ballooning: For a truly unique experience, consider taking a hot air balloon ride over the Yarra Valley. From high above, you'll get panoramic views of the vineyards, hills, and forests, all while enjoying the peaceful calm of the early morning sky.

Best Time to Visit

Autumn (March to May): This is one of the best times to visit the Yarra Valley, as the vineyards transform with autumn colors. It's also harvest season, so there's a vibrant energy around the wineries.

Spring (September to November): Spring offers mild temperatures and blooming vines, making it another great time to visit.

Summer (December to February): The warmer weather is perfect for enjoying outdoor wine tastings and meals, though it can get crowded during peak holiday seasons.

How to Get There

The Yarra Valley is easily accessible from Melbourne, located about 60 to 90 minutes by car. You can either rent a car or join a guided tour, which is highly recommended for those who want to relax and enjoy wine tastings without worrying about driving. Many tour companies offer full-day tours that include visits to several wineries, lunch, and transport, making it easy to explore the best of the region.

Phillip Island Penguin Parade

Why Visit the Phillip Island Penguin Parade?

Phillip Island is renowned for its rich wildlife and stunning coastal landscapes, but its Penguin Parade is the star attraction. Every evening, as the sun sets, hundreds of Little Penguins waddle from the ocean back to their burrows along the island's coastline. This spectacular sight, known as the Penguin Parade, offers a rare opportunity to witness these adorable creatures in their natural habitat.

Highlights of the Penguin Parade Experience

Penguin Parade Viewing: As dusk falls, the Little Penguins begin to emerge from the sea in groups, making their way to the sand dunes. You can watch them from elevated viewing platforms along the coastline, providing an unobstructed view of the parade as they waddle to their burrows. The penguins typically return to the shore between sunset and dark, and the parade continues for about an hour.

Penguin Discovery Centre: Located at the Penguin Parade site, the **Penguin Discovery Centre** offers an educational experience about the life cycle and behavior of the Little Penguins. Interactive displays and informative talks provide insights into the conservation efforts being made to protect the penguin colony and the island's unique ecosystem.

Penguin Parade Rangers: As part of your experience, rangers offer informative talks about the penguins, their habits, and the island's natural environment. These experts share fascinating facts and help you understand the significance of the Penguin Parade, ensuring you get the most out of your visit.

Wildlife Viewing: Besides penguins, Phillip Island is home to other fascinating wildlife. The island is also known for its colonies of **seals**, **koalas**, and **kangaroos**. You can visit the **Koala Conservation Centre** or explore the island's scenic coastline for more wildlife encounters.

Photography Opportunities: The Penguin Parade provides ample opportunities for memorable photos, especially as the penguins emerge from the surf and march across the beach. While photography is not allowed during the parade itself to avoid disturbing the penguins, the stunning coastal landscapes offer fantastic photo opportunities before and after the event.

How to Get There

Phillip Island is easily accessible from Melbourne by car or through organized tours. The most scenic route is to drive via the **South Gippsland Highway**, which takes approximately 90 minutes to reach the island. Alternatively, you can join a guided day tour from Melbourne that includes transport, entry to the Penguin Parade, and a visit to other local attractions.

Best Time to Visit

Summer (December to February): During summer, the Penguin Parade is most popular, and you'll have the chance to see the penguins in their breeding season. However, it can be more crowded.

Autumn and Spring (March to May, September to November): These seasons offer a quieter, more peaceful experience. The weather is mild, and the penguins still perform their nightly parade.

Winter (June to August): While the weather is cooler, winter is also a great time to see the penguins. The crowds are smaller, but the penguins still march in large numbers, and the winter skies often provide dramatic backdrops.

Tips for Visiting the Penguin Parade

Dress Warmly: It can get chilly in the evening, especially by the coast, so make sure to bring a jacket and wear comfortable clothing for walking.

Arrive Early: While the Penguin Parade typically starts after dark, arriving early ensures you get a good spot on the viewing platforms. The site is popular, and it can get crowded, so securing a good spot is important for a better experience.

Respect the Penguins: To protect the penguins and their habitat, visitors are asked to avoid using flash photography or making loud noises that could disturb the wildlife.

Be Patient: The penguins typically emerge at dusk, so be prepared to wait. The parade may last up to an hour, and while the penguins are adorable, they do take their time making their way to their burrows.

Tasmania Day Trips

1. Port Arthur Historic Site

Located just 1.5 hours from Hobart, **Port Arthur** is a UNESCO World Heritage site and one of Tasmania's most significant historic landmarks. Once a notorious penal colony, the site now offers a glimpse into Australia's convict past through well-preserved buildings and haunting ruins.

Highlights: The historic prison, the haunting **Isle of the Dead** cemetery, and scenic harbor views.

Best for: History enthusiasts and those interested in Australia's convict heritage.

2. Mount Field National Park

Only a 1.5-hour drive from Hobart, **Mount Field National Park** is a stunning natural destination. The park offers a variety of trails that take you through lush forests, past stunning waterfalls, and up to the alpine peaks of Mount Field.

Highlights: **Russell Falls**, a picturesque 3-tier waterfall; **Lake Dobson** for alpine views; and a range of easy to moderate walks.

Best for: Hikers and nature lovers looking for diverse landscapes in a short amount of time.

3. Freycinet National Park

Freycinet National Park, about 2.5 hours' drive from Hobart, is one of Tasmania's most iconic natural attractions. It's home to some of Australia's most beautiful beaches, including the famous **Wineglass Bay**.

Highlights: The breathtaking view from the **Wineglass Bay Lookout**, beach walks, and crystal-clear waters perfect for swimming.

Best for: Coastal scenery, photography, and those looking to explore Tasmania's famous beaches.

4. Bruny Island

A short ferry ride from Hobart, **Bruny Island** is a haven for foodies, nature lovers, and wildlife enthusiasts. The island is known for its dramatic cliffs, pristine beaches, and local gourmet produce.

Highlights: **Bruny Island Cheese Company**, the **Bruny Island Neck Lookout**, and the chance to spot wildlife such as **seals**, **whales**, and **birdlife**.

Best for: Those looking for a mix of nature, wildlife, and local food experiences.

5. Cradle Mountain-Lake St Clair National Park

Though Cradle Mountain is about a 4-hour drive from Hobart, it's worth the journey for a day trip, especially for hiking enthusiasts. The park is a UNESCO World Heritage-listed site known for its stunning landscapes, including rugged mountains, glacial lakes, and temperate rainforests.

Highlights: The famous **Cradle Mountain** hike, the tranquil **Dove Lake**, and a range of other trails with varying difficulty.

Best for: Hikers and outdoor adventurers looking for a more remote and immersive Tasmanian experience.

6. Bay of Fires

Located on Tasmania's northeast coast, **Bay of Fires** is famous for its white-sand beaches and vibrant orange lichen-covered rocks. It's a 2.5-hour drive from Launceston and a perfect destination for a scenic day trip.

Highlights: The stunning beaches, clear turquoise waters, and unique rock formations.

Best for: Beach lovers, photographers, and those seeking tranquility in a natural setting.

7. Launceston and Tamar Valley Wine Region

For a mix of culture, food, and history, a day trip to **Launceston** and the **Tamar Valley** is ideal. Just 30 minutes from the city, the Tamar Valley is Tasmania's premier wine region, known for its cool-climate wines and picturesque vineyards.

Highlights: Wine tasting at local vineyards, exploring the historic **Cataract Gorge**, and visiting local farms and markets.

Best for: Wine lovers and those who appreciate a mix of nature and culture.

8. Huon Valley

Just a 40-minute drive from Hobart, the **Huon Valley** offers a peaceful escape into Tasmania's rural heart. Known for its apple orchards and wilderness, the Huon Valley is perfect for those looking to enjoy nature, food, and local produce.

Highlights: Tahune Airwalk, scenic river views, and local produce such as apples, berries, and fresh seafood.

Best for: Those seeking a more relaxed day out, food enthusiasts, and nature lovers.

9. Maria Island

Accessible by ferry from Triabunna (about 1.5 hours' drive from Hobart), **Maria Island** is a beautiful, largely undeveloped island known for its pristine beaches, wildlife, and historical ruins.

Highlights: Walking trails with views of wildlife like **wallabies** and **koalas**, **Darlington** settlement ruins, and dramatic coastal cliffs.

Best for: Nature lovers, wildlife watchers, and history enthusiasts.

10. St Helens and the East Coast

St Helens, located on Tasmania's east coast, is a charming coastal town with some of the state's most spectacular beaches. It's a 2.5-hour drive from Launceston and provides easy access to beautiful natural landscapes.

Highlights: **The Bay of Fires Conservation Area**, the **Tarkine** wilderness, and water activities such as kayaking and fishing.

Best for: Beach lovers and those seeking outdoor activities like hiking, kayaking, and fishing.

Chapter 13: 7-Day Classic Australia Itinerary

Day 1: Arrival in Sydney

Morning: Arrival and Introduction to Sydney

Activities:

Upon arrival at Sydney Airport, take a moment to freshen up and get oriented with the city. Consider getting an **Opal Card** for easy access to public transport (buses, trains, ferries, and light rail). It's the best way to navigate Sydney, as it offers affordable travel options with a pay-as-you-go system.

If you're feeling jetlagged, you can relax and get your bearings at your hotel, whether you've chosen a spot near **Circular Quay** for harbor views or closer to **Bondi Beach** for a coastal vibe.

Consider taking a short stroll to **Circular Quay** to experience the harbor views, the Sydney Opera House, and **Sydney Harbour Bridge** from the ground. This will also allow you to get used to the surrounding area.

Breakfast:

Head to **The Grounds of Alexandria** (Open from 7:00 AM - 3:00 PM) for a relaxed breakfast experience. A popular choice for tourists and locals alike, you can try their famous **smashed avocado toast** with poached eggs, or a hearty **eggs benedict**. A freshly brewed coffee here is a must to start your day.

Price: Approximately AUD 20-30 for breakfast per person.

Mid-Morning: Explore Iconic Sydney Landmarks

Activities:

Walk to the **Royal Botanic Garden** (free entry), which opens at 7:00 AM. This expansive garden near the Opera House offers lush greenery and stunning views of the Sydney Harbour. It's perfect for a peaceful walk to shake off any jet lag.

Sydney Opera House Tour (9:00 AM - 5:00 PM): Consider a guided tour to learn about the history of this iconic building. The standard tour costs around AUD 42 for adults.

Afternoon: Sydney Harbour and Darling Harbour

Activities:

Take a **Sydney Harbour Ferry** (Operates every 30 minutes) from **Circular Quay** to **Manly Beach** (Approx. 30 minutes). Enjoy the spectacular harbor views as you pass by the Opera House, Harbour Bridge, and upscale waterfront neighborhoods.

After arriving at **Manly Beach**, you can relax by the beach or take a short walk to **Manly Corso** for a stroll through boutique shops and cafes.

Lunch:

For lunch, head to **Hugos Manly** (Open from 11:00 AM - 3:00 PM). Try their famous wood-fired pizza or fresh seafood options while enjoying the relaxed beach atmosphere.

Price: Around AUD 25-40 per person.

Mid-Afternoon: Visit Darling Harbour

Activities:

After returning to the city, head to **Darling Harbour** for a variety of attractions such as the **Australian National Maritime Museum** (Open 9:30 AM - 5:00 PM; Entry AUD 25), or simply enjoy a stroll around the waterfront.

If you have time, visit **SEA LIFE Sydney Aquarium** (Open 9:30 AM - 7:00 PM; Entry AUD 40) to see the vibrant marine life of Australia.

Evening: Sunset at Sydney Harbour

Activities:

Head to **Mrs. Macquarie's Chair** (Open until sunset), located in the Royal Botanic Garden, to catch an iconic Sydney sunset with sweeping views of the Harbour Bridge and Opera House. It's an excellent spot for photos.

If you're feeling adventurous, try the **BridgeClimb** (Operates 8:00 AM - 5:00 PM, Climb takes around 3 hours; AUD 198 per person) to the top of the Sydney Harbour Bridge for panoramic views of the city. Booking in advance is recommended.

Dinner:

For dinner, dine at **Quay Restaurant** (Open 5:30 PM - 10:30 PM) in Circular Quay, offering world-class Australian cuisine with an unparalleled view of Sydney Harbour. You could try the signature **8-course degustation menu** (AUD 225), or opt for an à la carte experience.

Alternatively, head to **The Rocks** area for a more casual, yet delicious meal at **The Glenmore Hotel** (Open until late). Enjoy their hearty **fish and chips** or a delicious **steak** with a view of the Sydney Harbour Bridge.

Price for Quay: Around AUD 200 per person for a fine-dining experience.

Night: Sydney's Nightlife

Activities:

After dinner, explore **The Rocks** for vibrant nightlife. Visit **The Fortune of War** (Sydney's oldest pub) or head to **Opera Bar** for cocktails while enjoying the view of the Opera House lit up at night.

If you're into late-night entertainment, check out **The Star Casino** or **Sydney's rooftop bars** such as **The Old Clare Hotel** or **Sydney Tower Eye's Sky Lounge**.

Getting Around Options:

Public Transport: Trains, buses, and ferries are the most convenient ways to get around. An **Opal Card** is your best option for transport.

Taxi or Ride-sharing: Services like **Uber** and **Ola** are also widely available for shorter trips or late-night transportation.

Summary of Costs:

Breakfast at The Grounds of Alexandria: AUD 20-30

Sydney Opera House Tour: AUD 42

Lunch at Hugos Manly: AUD 25-40

Ferry to Manly: AUD 8.50 one-way

Attractions (Museums, Aquarium, BridgeClimb, etc.): AUD 25-40 each

Dinner at Quay Restaurant: AUD 200 per person

Day 2: Sydney Exploration

Morning: Discover Sydney's Rich History and Culture

Activities:

Start your day with a visit to **The Art Gallery of New South Wales** (Open 10:00 AM - 5:00 PM, free entry), located in The Domain. It's one of the most significant public galleries in Australia, showcasing a rich collection of Australian, European, and Asian art.

Afterward, take a short walk to **Hyde Park** for a peaceful stroll around the city's oldest park. Stop by **St. Mary's Cathedral**, located at the park's southern end (Open 6:00 AM - 6:00 PM), to admire its stunning Gothic architecture.

Breakfast:

Head to **Bourke Street Bakery** (Open from 7:00 AM), one of Sydney's best-loved bakeries. You can try their **famous ricotta and spinach pastry** or a **croissant** paired with a flat white coffee. It's a great way to start your morning.

Price: AUD 10-20 for breakfast.

Mid-Morning: Visit the Historic Rocks Area

Activities:

Explore **The Rocks** district, Sydney's historic heart, which offers a blend of cobblestone lanes, markets, and cultural heritage. The **Rocks Discovery Museum** (Open 10:00 AM - 5:00 PM; free entry) gives insight into the area's rich colonial history and Aboriginal significance.

Don't miss the **Sydney Harbour Bridge** Pylon Lookout (Open 10:00 AM - 5:00 PM; Entry AUD 19), where you can learn about the bridge's history and enjoy stunning views of the harbor.

Lunch: Tasty and Casual Dining

Activities:

After immersing yourself in history, head to **The Glenmore Hotel** in The Rocks for lunch (Open 12:00 PM - 2:30 PM). The rooftop offers panoramic views of the

Harbour Bridge, making it a great spot to enjoy casual fare. Consider ordering a **burger with fries** or a **seafood platter**.

Price: AUD 25-40 per person.

Afternoon: Nature and Adventure

Activities:

Take a ferry to **Taronga Zoo** (Open 9:30 AM - 5:00 PM; Entry AUD 49). Located on the shores of Sydney Harbour, it's home to native Australian wildlife as well as exotic species. The zoo offers incredible views of the Sydney skyline and is a great spot for animal lovers.

Alternatively, visit **Bondi Beach** (via bus or train) for an afternoon swim or coastal walk. The **Bondi to Coogee Coastal Walk** (about 6 km, around 2 hours) offers spectacular cliffside views and beautiful beaches along the way.

Mid-Afternoon: Sydney's Beautiful Beaches

Activities:

If you opt for **Bondi Beach**, enjoy some time in the sun and sand, then grab an ice cream from **Gelato Messina** on the main strip for a treat. Or you can check out the **Bondi Markets** (Open 9:00 AM - 3:00 PM on Sundays) for handmade goods and local produce.

For a quieter experience, head to **Bronte Park** and enjoy a relaxed afternoon by the beach. This is a lesser-known gem just south of Bondi, offering an intimate, less crowded vibe.

Dinner: Fine Dining or Seafood Feast

Activities:

In the evening, you have two excellent options depending on your mood.

For a **fine-dining experience**, head to **Bennelong Restaurant** (located inside the Sydney Opera House; Open 5:30 PM - 9:00 PM). This is one of Sydney's best dining spots, offering a seasonal Australian menu with a fine wine selection and unbeatable views of the harbor. Try the **barramundi** or the **saltbush lamb**.

Price: AUD 150-200 per person.

For a more relaxed seafood dinner, visit **Sydney Fish Market** (Open 5:00 AM - 3:00 PM), a local institution where you can try fresh seafood platters or sushi at various market stalls. It's a great spot for seafood lovers looking for a casual meal.

Price: AUD 25-40 per person.

Night: Experience Sydney's Nightlife

Activities:

For a laid-back evening, enjoy cocktails at **Opera Bar** (Open 12:00 PM - Late). With an amazing view of the Opera House and Sydney Harbour Bridge, it's the perfect place to unwind after a busy day of sightseeing.

Alternatively, you can explore the vibrant nightlife scene in **King's Cross**. Head to a trendy bar like **The Roosevelt** or a nightclub like **The Ivy** for a lively Sydney nightlife experience.

If you're into live music, check out **The Basement** (Open 7:00 PM onwards), which is one of Sydney's iconic live music venues. Expect performances from jazz to rock bands.

Getting Around Options:

Public Transport: Utilize your **Opal Card** for easy access to buses, trains, ferries, and light rail. Sydney's public transport system is well connected and efficient, making it easy to get around.

Walking: Sydney is a very walkable city, and many major attractions are close to each other. Walking will allow you to soak in the sights at your own pace.

Taxi or Ride-sharing: Uber and **Ola** are available for shorter trips or if you need a more direct route.

Summary of Costs:

Breakfast at Bourke Street Bakery: AUD 10-20

Art Gallery of New South Wales: Free entry

Sydney Harbour Bridge Pylon Lookout: AUD 19

Lunch at The Glenmore Hotel: AUD 25-40

Taronga Zoo Entry: AUD 49

Bondi to Coogee Coastal Walk: Free

Dinner at Bennelong Restaurant: AUD 150-200

Drinks at Opera Bar or The Basement: AUD 15-30

Day 3: Fly to Cairns & Great Barrier Reef

Morning: Flight to Cairns

Activities:

Flight to Cairns: Start your day early and catch a morning flight from Sydney to **Cairns**. The flight is about 3 hours, so plan for an early departure (around 7:00 AM). Book a flight with **Qantas** or **Jetstar** for the best options. You'll arrive at Cairns Airport by around 9:00 AM.

Once you land, grab your luggage, and you can either take a **taxi** or **Shuttle Bus** to your hotel in Cairns. The **Sunlover Holidays** airport shuttle (AUD 18-25) is an affordable option. Alternatively, ride-sharing services like **Uber** are available.

Breakfast:

Breakfast at Cairns: Upon arrival, head to **Caffiend** (Open 6:30 AM - 3:00 PM), a popular local café for a great breakfast. Opt for their delicious **sweetcorn fritters** or a **classic Aussie breakfast** with bacon, eggs, and avocado toast.

Price: AUD 15-25 per person.

Mid-Morning: Cairns Esplanade and Lagoon

Activities:

After settling in, take a stroll along the **Cairns Esplanade** (a 10-minute walk from the city center). This area is known for its scenic views, parks, and waterfront promenade. You can enjoy the **Cairns Esplanade Lagoon** (free entry, open daily 6:00 AM - 9:00 PM), a man-made lagoon where you can relax, swim, or enjoy a peaceful walk by the ocean.

You can also explore **Cairns Regional Gallery** (Open 10:00 AM - 5:00 PM; Free entry for members, AUD 6 for general admission), which offers a great insight into the local art scene.

Lunch:

Lunch at Salt House (Open 11:30 AM - 3:00 PM): Situated along the Esplanade with stunning views of the marina, **Salt House** offers a great place for lunch. Try their fresh **seafood platter** or a **grilled barramundi**.

Price: AUD 25-45 per person.

Afternoon: Great Barrier Reef Day Trip

Activities:

After lunch, prepare for an afternoon trip to the **Great Barrier Reef**, one of the world's most famous natural wonders. The best way to experience it is through a **reef tour** or **scuba diving** day trip.

Book a tour with **Quicksilver Cruises** or **Reef Magic Cruises** (both departs from **Cairns Marina**). Most tours start around **12:30 PM - 1:00 PM** and last for 5-7 hours. These tours will take you to the outer reef, where you can snorkel, dive, or simply enjoy the coral views from a glass-bottom boat.

Reef Tour Price: Around **AUD 200-250** for a snorkeling tour, and **AUD 300+** for diving options.

Mid-Afternoon: Reef Exploration

Activities:

Spend your afternoon snorkeling or diving in the crystal-clear waters of the Great Barrier Reef. If you're not into diving, a glass-bottom boat ride is an excellent option to witness the marine life without getting wet. You'll likely see **tropical fish**, **sea turtles**, and **colorful corals**.

Some tours include a **Marine Biologist talk** about the reef's biodiversity, giving you a deeper understanding of the environment you're exploring.

Evening: Return to Cairns & Relax

Activities:

After an exhilarating afternoon on the Great Barrier Reef, return to Cairns by **5:00 PM - 6:00 PM**. Afterward, you can unwind and relax at your hotel or take a leisurely walk along the **Cairns Esplanade** at sunset.

If you're up for it, visit **Cairns Night Markets** (Open 5:00 PM - 10:00 PM) to shop for local crafts, souvenirs, and enjoy light snacks.

Dinner:

Dinner at Ochre Restaurant (Open 5:30 PM - 9:30 PM): Enjoy modern Australian cuisine with a focus on native ingredients at **Ochre**, one of Cairns' top fine dining spots. Try their **wallaby fillet** or a **barramundi** dish, both of which are specialties of the restaurant.

Price: AUD 40-70 per person.

Night: Cairns Nightlife

Activities:

If you're still feeling energetic after dinner, head to **Cairns' nightlife hub**, which includes vibrant spots like **The Woolshed** or **Rattle n Hum**, both offering a laid-back atmosphere with live music, drinks, and local vibes.

Alternatively, enjoy a relaxing evening at **The Reef Hotel Casino** (Open from 10:00 AM), where you can try your luck or simply enjoy the lounges and bars.

Getting Around Options:

Public Transport: Cairns is compact, and most attractions are within walking distance. If you need to get further, **local buses** are available, or taxis and **Uber** are popular choices.

Cycling: Cairns is a very bike-friendly city, and many places offer bike rentals to explore the area at your own pace.

Shuttle/Transfers for Reef Tour: For your Great Barrier Reef excursion, shuttle transfers are usually included in your tour package.

Summary of Costs:

Flight from Sydney to Cairns: Around AUD 100-200 one-way

Breakfast at Caffiend: AUD 15-25

Cairns Esplanade Lagoon: Free

Lunch at Salt House: AUD 25-45

Great Barrier Reef Tour (Snorkeling): AUD 200-250

Dinner at Ochre Restaurant: AUD 40-70

Cairns Night Markets: Free entry, snacks and souvenirs around AUD 5-20

Day 4: Daintree Rainforest & Cape Tribulation

Morning: Journey to the Daintree Rainforest

Activities:

Begin your day early with a hearty breakfast and prepare for a full day of nature exploration. Your adventure will start with a drive from Cairns to the **Daintree Rainforest** (about a 2-hour drive). You can either drive yourself or join a guided tour. If you're driving, take the **Captain Cook Highway**, which offers scenic views along the way.

If you opt for a **guided tour**, choose a reputable operator like **Daintree Discovery Tours** or **Daintree Eco Safaris** (Tours typically depart around **7:30 AM - 8:00 AM**). Tours usually include a visit to **Mossman Gorge** and a nature walk through the rainforest.

Breakfast:

Breakfast at the hotel or a nearby café like **Café China** in Cairns (Open from 7:00 AM) for a quick and light breakfast. Try an **acai bowl** or **eggs on toast** with coffee to energize you for the adventure ahead.

Price: AUD 10-20.

Mid-Morning: Mossman Gorge & Rainforest Walk

Activities:

Your first stop is **Mossman Gorge**, located just outside the Daintree Rainforest. You'll enjoy a **guided rainforest walk** with an Indigenous guide (Open from 9:00 AM - 4:00 PM). This UNESCO-listed heritage area is known for its lush tropical rainforest, crystal-clear streams, and ancient trees.

The **Mossman Gorge Centre** offers an informative cultural experience, providing insight into the area's heritage and Indigenous culture (Entry: AUD 10 for the Gorge shuttle and walk).

Lunch:

Lunch at the Daintree Rainforest: After your walk, stop at **Daintree Tea House Restaurant** (Open 11:30 AM - 2:30 PM) for a refreshing lunch. Known for using local produce, you can try their **wild-caught barramundi** or **tropical fruit salad**.

Price: AUD 20-40 per person.

Afternoon: Cape Tribulation

Activities:

After lunch, head further north to **Cape Tribulation**, where the rainforest meets the reef (about 30-45 minutes from Mossman Gorge). Explore the pristine beaches, take a dip, or just relax on the shore. Cape Tribulation is known for its secluded beauty, offering a peaceful atmosphere surrounded by natural wonders.

You can also explore the **Cape Tribulation Beach** or take a walk along the **Dubiji Boardwalk** (Open 24/7, free entry), where you'll see the rainforest extending all the way to the ocean.

For a unique experience, join a **Daintree River Cruise** (usually starting at **1:30 PM - 2:00 PM**), where you'll have the chance to spot **saltwater crocodiles**, **birdlife**, and other wildlife along the river.

Mid-Afternoon: Daintree Ice Cream Company

Activities:

Treat yourself to something sweet by visiting the **Daintree Ice Cream Company** (Open 10:00 AM - 5:00 PM), located in the heart of the rainforest. They offer a variety of tropical fruit-flavored ice creams made from local ingredients like **mango**, **soursop**, **coconut**, and **wattle seed**.

Price: AUD 8-12 for a cone or cup.

Evening: Return to Cairns

Activities:

After exploring Cape Tribulation, start making your way back to Cairns (around 2 hours by car). If you're on a tour, your guide will drive you back to your accommodation.

If time permits, stop at **Port Douglas** for a short evening stroll along **Four Mile Beach**, or explore the local shops and bars in this charming coastal town.

Dinner:

Dinner at the Dockside Café (Open 5:30 PM - 9:00 PM), located on the Cairns Marina, is an excellent choice for a relaxed evening meal. Try their **grilled fish of the day** or **steak with garlic butter**.

Price: AUD 25-45 per person.

Night: Relax in Cairns

After returning from your Daintree and Cape Tribulation adventure, take a relaxing evening walk along **Cairns Esplanade** or enjoy some drinks at **The Pier Bar**, located on the Cairns waterfront (Open 10:00 AM - 12:00 AM).

Alternatively, spend the evening at **Cairns Night Markets** (Open 5:00 PM - 10:00 PM), where you can pick up some unique souvenirs or just enjoy the lively atmosphere.

Getting Around Options:

Self-drive: Renting a car is the best option for exploring Daintree Rainforest and Cape Tribulation at your own pace. The drive is scenic and well-maintained.

Guided Tour: If you prefer a more informative experience, a guided tour is highly recommended, as local guides provide valuable knowledge about the area's natural and cultural history.

Daintree River Cruise: This tour is often included in the guided trips or can be booked separately at the river.

Summary of Costs:

Breakfast at Café China: AUD 10-20

Mossman Gorge Entry and Shuttle: AUD 10

Lunch at Daintree Tea House Restaurant: AUD 20-40

Daintree River Cruise: AUD 30-50

Ice Cream at Daintree Ice Cream Company: AUD 8-12

Dinner at Dockside Café: AUD 25-45

Guided Tour of Daintree & Cape Tribulation (if applicable): AUD 150-250

Day 5: Fly to Melbourne

Morning: Flight to Melbourne

Activities:

After a memorable time in Cairns, head to Cairns Airport for your flight to **Melbourne**. The flight duration is about 3 hours. Morning flights usually depart between **7:00 AM and 9:00 AM**, so ensure you're packed and ready for an early start.

Once you arrive in Melbourne (around **10:30 AM - 11:00 AM**), take a **taxi**, **SkyBus**, or **Uber** to your hotel. **SkyBus** is a convenient option for airport transfers, costing about **AUD 19** one-way and taking around 20-30 minutes to the city center.

Breakfast:

Breakfast at Melbourne Airport or the hotel: If you didn't have breakfast at the airport, you can stop by **Aromas Café** at Melbourne Airport (Open from 6:00 AM). Alternatively, your hotel will likely offer a continental breakfast.

Price: AUD 10-20

Mid-Morning: Federation Square and National Gallery of Victoria (NGV)

Activities:

After arriving in Melbourne and checking in at your hotel, head to **Federation Square**, a cultural precinct in the heart of Melbourne. It's a great place to explore iconic attractions, and it's easily accessible by foot or tram.

Visit the **National Gallery of Victoria (NGV)** (Open 10:00 AM - 5:00 PM, free entry). This world-class art museum houses an impressive collection of both Australian and international art. Don't miss their renowned **Indigenous Art** and **European Art** collections.

Admission: Free for permanent collections; special exhibitions may charge an entry fee (AUD 15-25).

Lunch:

Lunch at Federation Square or nearby: There are many dining options in Federation Square. Head to **Beer DeLuxe** (Open 11:30 AM - 10:00 PM) for a great meal with an Australian touch. Try their **barramundi burger** or a **beef pie** with chips.

Price: AUD 20-30 per person.

Afternoon: Explore Melbourne Laneways and Hosier Lane

Activities:

Melbourne is famous for its laneways, and **Hosier Lane** is one of the most iconic. This alleyway is known for its vibrant street art and graffiti-covered walls. Spend the afternoon exploring Melbourne's laneways, including **AC/DC Lane** and **Degraves Street**, where you'll find quirky cafes, boutiques, and murals.

While in the area, visit **Block Arcade** (Open 9:00 AM - 6:00 PM), a historic shopping arcade with beautiful Victorian architecture. It's the perfect place to do some shopping or just enjoy the atmosphere.

Mid-Afternoon: Melbourne Skydeck

Activities:

Visit the **Eureka Skydeck** (Open 10:00 AM - 10:00 PM), located on the 88th floor of the Eureka Tower, for panoramic views of Melbourne. The Skydeck offers breathtaking views of the city's skyline, the Yarra River, and beyond. Don't miss the **Edge Experience**, where you can stand in a glass cube that extends from the building, offering a thrilling experience.

Admission: AUD 25 for adults, **Edge Experience** extra AUD 12.

Evening: Southbank and Dinner by the Yarra River

Activities:

After your Skydeck visit, head to the **Southbank Promenade**, a lively area along the Yarra River filled with restaurants, bars, and cultural venues. Enjoy a relaxing evening by the river with views of the Melbourne skyline.

You can also visit the **Melbourne Arts Precinct**, where you'll find cultural venues like **The Melbourne Recital Centre** or **Arts Centre Melbourne** (Check schedules for live performances).

Dinner:

Dinner at Chin Chin (Open 5:00 PM - 10:00 PM): For an unforgettable dining experience, head to **Chin Chin**, one of Melbourne's top restaurants serving modern Thai food. Try their **massaman curry** or **pad Thai** for a flavorful experience.

Price: AUD 30-50 per person.

Night: Enjoy Melbourne's Nightlife

Activities:

After dinner, you can explore **Melbourne's nightlife**, known for its vibrant bars, pubs, and cocktail lounges. Visit **The Everleigh** in Fitzroy (Open 6:00 PM - 2:00 AM), an intimate and stylish cocktail bar, or check out **Rooftop Bar** for stunning views and a relaxed atmosphere (Open 12:00 PM - 3:00 AM).

If you're interested in live music, check out **The Night Cat** in Fitzroy (Open from 7:00 PM), a venue known for its jazz, soul, and funk performances.

Getting Around Options:

Trams: Melbourne's **tram system** is one of the best ways to get around the city. You can use a **Myki card** to pay for tram, bus, and train travel. Trams are free in the **Central Business District (CBD)**, so it's easy to hop on and off when exploring.

Walking: Many of Melbourne's major attractions, like Federation Square, Hosier Lane, and Southbank, are within walking distance from each other, making walking a great option.

Bike Rentals: Melbourne also offers bike rentals, and there are several **hire stations** around the city for a fun way to explore.

Summary of Costs:

Flight from Cairns to Melbourne: AUD 100-200 one-way

Breakfast at Aromas Café: AUD 10-20

National Gallery of Victoria (NGV): Free for permanent collections

Lunch at Beer DeLuxe: AUD 20-30

Eureka Skydeck Admission: AUD 25

Dinner at Chin Chin: AUD 30-50

Drinks at Rooftop Bar: AUD 15-25

Day 6: Melbourne Day Trips

Morning: Great Ocean Road Adventure

Activities:

Start your day early, as the **Great Ocean Road** is a must-do day trip from Melbourne. This scenic drive offers breathtaking coastal views and a chance to see some of Australia's most famous landmarks, such as the **Twelve Apostles**.

The drive to the **Twelve Apostles** takes around **3 hours** from Melbourne, so it's recommended to either rent a car or join a **guided tour** (e.g., with **AAT Kings** or **Great Ocean Road Tours**), which departs around **7:30 AM - 8:00 AM**.

Along the way, stop at other iconic spots, including **Torquay**, **Bells Beach**, **Lorne**, and **Apollo Bay**, which offer coastal views, great beaches, and charming towns. If you're driving, take breaks at these picturesque spots for photos and a leisurely stroll.

Breakfast:

Breakfast at the hotel or a café before the trip. If you're departing from Melbourne early, grab a quick bite at **Hardware Société** (Open from 7:00 AM), known for their delicious **eggs benedict** and **French toast**.

Price: AUD 15-25.

Mid-Morning: Twelve Apostles & Loch Ard Gorge

Activities:

The **Twelve Apostles**, located in **Port Campbell National Park**, is the highlight of the Great Ocean Road. The rugged limestone stacks stand tall against the Southern Ocean. It's best to visit early in the day to avoid the crowds. The **visitor center** provides insightful displays about the geological history of the area (Open from **9:00 AM - 5:00 PM**).

Next, head to **Loch Ard Gorge** (about a 5-minute drive from the Twelve Apostles), another stunning coastal feature. This site is rich in history, named after the shipwreck of the Loch Ard in 1878. Take the short walk to the beach or the lookout for spectacular views.

Admission: Free (some parking fees may apply at certain spots).

Lunch:

Lunch at Apollo Bay: After spending the morning at the Twelve Apostles and Loch Ard Gorge, stop at **Apollo Bay** for lunch. Try **The Apollo Bay Hotel** (Open 12:00 PM - 2:30 PM) for a hearty **seafood platter** or **grilled fish**.

Price: AUD 20-35 per person.

Afternoon: Otway Rainforest & London Arch

Activities:

Continue your Great Ocean Road adventure with a visit to the **Otway Rainforest**, which is part of the **Great Otway National Park**. Take a **short walk** through the lush rainforest and see the towering trees, ferns, and diverse wildlife (Entrance: Free).

Next, visit **London Arch** (formerly known as London Bridge), a natural rock formation that was once an archway until part of it collapsed in 1990. The area is perfect for photos and offers an easy walk from the car park.

London Arch is located about **30 minutes** from Apollo Bay, and it's an easy stop before heading back to Melbourne.

Mid-Afternoon: Return to Melbourne

Activities:

After a full day of exploring, begin your drive back to Melbourne (approximately **3 hours**). If you're on a guided tour, you'll likely return around **5:30 PM** to **6:00 PM**.

Along the way, if you still have some energy, stop at **Torquay** for a quick coffee break or enjoy a sunset view over the beach before heading back to the city.

Evening: Relax and Unwind in Melbourne

Activities:

After returning to Melbourne, relax and take in the evening atmosphere. Consider walking along **Southbank Promenade**, where you can enjoy the view of the Yarra River with the city skyline.

If you're in the mood for some casual exploration, take a stroll through **Queen Victoria Market** (Open **6:00 AM - 3:00 PM**, closed Sundays), where you can shop for local goods, produce, and souvenirs. Even though the market may be closing by the time you arrive, the surrounding area is full of lively bars and restaurants.

Dinner:

Dinner at Huxtaburger (Open **5:00 PM - 10:00 PM**): After a long day trip, treat yourself to a tasty meal at **Huxtaburger** in Fitzroy. Enjoy an Australian-style **burger with chips** or a **vegetarian burger** paired with a cold beer.

Price: AUD 15-25 per person.

Night: Melbourne's Nightlife

Activities:

If you're not too tired from your day trip, Melbourne offers great nightlife options. Head to **Chin Chin** or **The Rooftop Bar** for a cocktail and views of the city's skyline. Alternatively, visit **Melbourne's laneways** for a more relaxed and atmospheric evening out.

For those interested in live music, **The Night Cat** or **Corner Hotel** offer some great performances, particularly in the **Fitzroy** and **Richmond** areas.

Getting Around Options:

Guided Tour: If you choose a guided tour, transportation is typically provided, making it a convenient and informative way to explore the Great Ocean Road. Tours often include pickup from your hotel in Melbourne.

Self-Drive: Renting a car gives you flexibility and control over your stops along the Great Ocean Road. Make sure to plan your route, as driving times can add up, especially if you want to explore multiple stops.

Public Transport: While public transport is available, it is less practical for this day trip due to the long distances. Renting a car or joining a tour is the best option.

Summary of Costs:

Great Ocean Road Tour (if guided): AUD 100-150 per person

Breakfast at Hardware Société: AUD 15-25

Lunch at The Apollo Bay Hotel: AUD 20-35

Eureka Skydeck Admission: Free

Dinner at Huxtaburger: AUD 15-25

Car Rental (if self-driving): AUD 50-100 per day

Day 7: Melbourne to Sydney and Departure

Morning: Travel from Melbourne to Sydney

Activities:

After a week of exploring Melbourne and its surrounding wonders, it's time to head back to **Sydney** for your return flight. Plan for an early morning flight, which will take about **1 hour and 30 minutes**. Flights typically depart from **Melbourne Airport (Tullamarine)** around **7:00 AM - 9:00 AM**.

After checking out of your hotel, take a taxi, **SkyBus**, or **Uber** to the airport. The **SkyBus** (AUD 19 one-way) is a convenient option for airport transfer, and the journey usually takes **20-30 minutes**.

Breakfast:

Breakfast at Melbourne Airport: If you're leaving early, grab a quick breakfast at **St. Ali Café** (Open from **5:00 AM**), known for its great coffee and breakfast options like **avocado toast** and **eggs on sourdough**.

Price: AUD 10-20.

Mid-Morning: Arrival in Sydney

Activities:

Upon arrival at **Sydney Airport**, take a **taxi**, **train**, or **Uber** to your hotel in **Sydney's CBD**. The **train** (Airport Link) takes about **13 minutes** and costs around **AUD 18**.

Once checked in, you can spend the remaining hours before your flight exploring a bit more of the city or doing some last-minute shopping.

Lunch:

Lunch at Circular Quay: For a scenic and delicious lunch, head to **Circular Quay**, where you'll find a variety of cafes and restaurants with views of the **Sydney Opera House** and **Harbour Bridge**. Try **Opera Bar** (Open from **11:00 AM - 10:00 PM**) for fresh **seafood** or a **burger with fries** while soaking in the views.

Price: AUD 20-40 per person.

Afternoon: Last-Minute Exploration (Optional)

Activities:

If time allows, you can take a stroll through **The Royal Botanic Garden**, which is just a short walk from Circular Quay. It's a perfect spot to relax, take some photos, and enjoy the lush greenery.

Alternatively, visit **The Rocks**, a historic area known for its cobblestone streets, boutique shops, and cafes. It's a great place to grab souvenirs or enjoy your last bit of Sydney's unique atmosphere.

If you want a view of the city before you depart, head to **Sydney Tower Eye** (Open **9:00 AM - 9:00 PM**). The observation deck offers panoramic views of the city for **AUD 29**.

Evening: Depart from Sydney

Activities:

After a short exploration, make your way back to the airport for your departure. Sydney's **Kingsford Smith Airport** is about **20-30 minutes** from the city center by **taxi** or **train**.

Ensure you arrive **2 hours before your international flight** (or **1 hour for domestic flights**).

Dinner (Optional, If Time Allows):

Dinner at the Airport: If you have time before your flight, you can grab a quick dinner at **The Bistro by SumoSalad** (Open **6:00 AM - 9:30 PM**) or **T1 International Dining**, where there are various food options, including sushi, sandwiches, and salads.

Price: AUD 15-25.

Getting Around:

Taxi: The most convenient option to travel from your hotel to the airport (AUD 40-60).

Train (Airport Link): A faster and cheaper option (AUD 18 one-way).

Uber: Reliable and convenient for airport transfers.

Summary of Costs:

Flight from Melbourne to Sydney: AUD 80-150 one-way

Breakfast at St. Ali Café: AUD 10-20

Lunch at Opera Bar: AUD 20-40

Sydney Tower Eye Admission: AUD 29

Taxi to Sydney Airport: AUD 40-60

Dinner at the Airport: AUD 15-25

Final Thoughts:

As your Australian adventure comes to a close, reflect on the incredible experiences you've had from the vibrant streets of Melbourne to the coastal beauty of the Great Ocean Road and the stunning Great Barrier Reef. With lasting memories and new discoveries, your time in Australia will surely stay with you long after your departure. Safe travels!

Chapter 14: Resources and Useful Links

Tourism Websites

1. Tourism Australia

Website: www.australia.com

Overview: As the official tourism website of Australia, this site is an essential resource for travelers. It offers detailed information on destinations, experiences, and events across the country. You can find guides for top attractions, itineraries, accommodation options, and tips for planning your trip.

Key Features:

Destination guides

Event listings and festival details

Interactive maps

Travel tips and suggested itineraries

2. Visit New South Wales

Website: www.visitnsw.com

Overview: This is the official site for tourism in New South Wales (NSW), home to iconic cities like Sydney. The website provides a wealth of information on things to do, where to stay, and where to eat in NSW, as well as itineraries and travel advice.

Key Features:

Sydney and regional NSW attractions

Seasonal travel tips and recommendations

Adventure and nature experiences in the Blue Mountains, Hunter Valley, and more

3. Queensland Tourism

Website: www.queensland.com

Overview: Focused on Queensland, one of Australia's most diverse regions, this site offers comprehensive details about destinations like the Great Barrier Reef, Gold Coast, and tropical rainforests. It also provides accommodation and travel planning tools.

Key Features:

Beach, reef, and nature experiences

Holiday packages and promotions

Events calendar

Adventure and family-friendly activities

4. Visit Victoria

Website: www.visitvictoria.com

Overview: This website provides in-depth information on Victoria, including Melbourne and the surrounding areas. It's a great resource for exploring everything from city attractions to vineyards and natural landscapes in the state's countryside.

Key Features:

Melbourne city highlights and cultural experiences

Wine regions, food, and local dining

Nature and outdoor experiences, including the Great Ocean Road

Travel itineraries

5. South Australia Tourism

Website: www.southaustralia.com

Overview: For those looking to explore South Australia, this website offers detailed travel information on cities like Adelaide and scenic regions like the Barossa Valley, Kangaroo Island, and the Flinders Ranges. The site is also a great resource for discovering festivals and events.

Key Features:

Detailed guides on wine, food, and local culture

Adventure and wildlife experiences

Major events and festivals

Outdoor activities and eco-tourism experiences

6. Tourism Northern Territory

Website: www.northernterritory.com

Overview: This site focuses on the Northern Territory, including destinations like Uluru, Alice Springs, and Kakadu National Park. It's the perfect resource for travelers seeking adventure, Indigenous culture, and dramatic landscapes.

Key Features:

Information on Uluru and Kata Tjuta

Aboriginal culture and heritage experiences

Wildlife and adventure tours

Outdoor and nature activities in the Outback

7. Tourism Tasmania

Website: www.discovertasmania.com

Overview: Tasmania is known for its wild beauty, and this website is a great place to start for planning your trip. It provides insights into Tasmania's wilderness, heritage sites, hiking trails, and eco-friendly travel options.

Key Features:

Information on Tasmania's national parks and World Heritage sites

Adventure tours and scenic drives

Sustainable travel tips

Arts, food, and local culture

8. Australian National Tourism Websites

Website: www.nationalparks.nsw.gov.au

Overview: For nature lovers, this website covers Australia's national parks and reserves, offering a range of outdoor experiences from bushwalking and camping to wildlife spotting. The site features parks from across New South Wales, including those in Sydney and beyond.

Key Features:

Hiking trails and camping locations

National park tours and educational programs

Wildlife watching opportunities

9. Australia's Official Events and Festivals Site

Website: www.australianfestivals.com.au

Overview: If you're visiting Australia for its vibrant arts and cultural scene, this site provides a list of events and festivals happening across the country. From music and film festivals to art exhibitions and local cultural celebrations, it's the go-to site for event planning.

Key Features:

Festival listings by state

Seasonal events and cultural celebrations

Special interest events like food and wine festivals

10. Lonely Planet Australia

Website: www.lonelyplanet.com/australia

Overview: Lonely Planet's Australia section provides expert advice, travel tips, and up-to-date guides on destinations, things to do, and practical information. It's an excellent resource for those looking for trusted insights into Australia's best attractions and hidden gems.

Key Features:

Destination guides with expert recommendations

Interactive maps and itineraries

Travel tips for planning your Australia trip

Emergency Services

1. Emergency Numbers

Australia uses a universal emergency number for most types of emergencies:

000 – This is the primary emergency number to call for police, fire, ambulance, and other urgent situations across Australia. It's free to call, and operators are available 24/7.

Police: For non-life-threatening crimes or situations that need police attention.

Ambulance: For medical emergencies, injuries, or illness.

Fire: For fires, rescues, and hazardous material situations.

2. Medical Emergencies

Australia has a high standard of medical care, and in the case of illness or injury, you can rely on local hospitals and clinics. If you need urgent medical attention:

Call 000 for ambulance services to take you to the nearest hospital.

In many cities, urgent care clinics or medical centers are available for non-emergency but urgent medical conditions.

Medicare: Australian residents are covered by the public health insurance system, Medicare. However, as a visitor, you may need to pay for medical services unless you have travel insurance that covers emergency medical expenses.

3. Fire and Natural Disasters

Australia is prone to bushfires, especially in the summer months, and extreme weather conditions like cyclones and floods:

Fire Emergency: Call **000** for immediate response or to report a bushfire.

State Emergency Service (SES): For flooding, storm damage, or other extreme weather conditions, you can contact the SES in each state. You can call **132 500** for assistance.

4. Police Services

Police in Australia are available for a variety of situations, including emergencies, crime, road accidents, and public safety concerns:

Call 000 for urgent police assistance (e.g., theft, assault, or disturbances).

For non-urgent matters, contact the local police station directly or visit the nearest police station for help with reporting an issue.

5. Poisoning and Toxicology

In the case of poisoning or exposure to toxic substances, you can contact:

Poisons Information Centre: Call **13 11 26** for immediate advice on poisoning and toxic exposure. This helpline is available 24/7.

6. Transport and Road Incidents

If you're involved in a car accident or need roadside assistance:

Roadside Assistance: Various companies offer services such as towing, tire changes, and emergency repairs. These include major providers like NRMA, RACV, RACQ, and others.

For accidents involving serious injury or property damage, call **000** for ambulance or police.

7. After-Hours Health Services

Many cities and towns offer after-hours clinics for medical issues that are not emergencies but require attention outside of normal office hours. You can find after-hours care options on local health service websites or through your accommodation concierge.

8. International Assistance

If you're traveling with a medical condition or require special assistance, contact your travel insurance provider. They often have 24/7 emergency hotlines that can help with arranging medical treatment, evacuations, or any other issues related to health and safety.

9. Travel Insurance Contacts

Before traveling, make sure to register your travel insurance with a 24-hour helpline number in case of emergencies. Your insurance may also cover costs for medical evacuation, canceled trips, or any unforeseen expenses due to emergencies.

Language Resources

1. Translation Apps

For travelers who don't speak English fluently, translation apps can be incredibly helpful in overcoming language barriers. Some of the most popular apps include:

Google Translate: A widely used app that translates text, speech, and even images in real time. It supports many languages and works offline after downloading language packs.

iTranslate: Offers translation for text and voice in over 100 languages, with an offline mode for convenience.

Microsoft Translator: This app provides translation for both text and speech and is useful for conversations in real-time.

2. Language Learning Apps

If you want to improve your English skills before or during your trip, several apps can help you practice speaking, listening, reading, and writing in English:

Duolingo: A fun and interactive app that helps you learn English and other languages through games and exercises.

Babbel: Offers structured lessons on various topics, from basics to more advanced language skills.

Memrise: Focuses on practical vocabulary and speaking skills to help you communicate in real-world situations.

3. English for Travel Books and Guides

If you prefer physical books, there are numerous English phrasebooks and travel guides available for different languages. These books can provide common phrases and expressions that are useful when navigating the country.

Lonely Planet Phrasebooks: These are available for many languages and provide essential phrases for travelers, including emergency words, directions, and common conversations.

Rick Steves' Language Guides: These guides offer simple travel phrases and tips on how to communicate effectively while traveling.

4. Local Language Schools and Classes

For those looking to improve their English in Australia, many language schools and institutions offer classes specifically tailored for non-native speakers. Here are some resources:

English Australia: A network of English language centers across the country that offers accredited English language courses for travelers.

TAFE (Technical and Further Education): Many TAFE institutions in Australia offer English as a Second Language (ESL) courses for international students.

Community Centers: Various community organizations and libraries provide free or low-cost English classes for immigrants and travelers.

5. Aussie Slang and Local Phrases

Australian English includes some unique slang and expressions that may be confusing to newcomers. Here are some commonly used terms:

Arvo: Afternoon

G'day: Hello

Macca's: McDonald's

No worries: It's okay / You're welcome

She'll be right: Everything will be fine

Bogan: An unsophisticated or unrefined person

Thongs: Flip-flops (footwear)

For travelers who want to familiarize themselves with Aussie slang, websites like **Aussie Slang Dictionary** or **The Australian National Dictionary** provide extensive lists and explanations.

6. Local Language Exchange Programs

If you're looking to practice your English with native speakers or meet people, you can join language exchange programs. Some options include:

Tandem: A language exchange app that connects learners with native speakers around the world.

Conversation Exchange: An online platform where you can find language partners in Australia to practice speaking English.

7. Tourist Information Centers

Tourist information centers in major Australian cities often have multilingual staff and can provide printed materials in different languages. These centers are a great resource for travelers who need help understanding the local language or directions.

8. Local Translation Services

In case of urgent need for professional translation or interpretation, Australia has certified translation services available. The **NAATI (National Accreditation Authority for Translators and Interpreters)** is the official accreditation body, and you can find professional translators and interpreters across the country who can assist in various languages.

9. English Language Radio and TV

Listening to local radio or watching Australian TV can help improve your understanding of the accent and local expressions. Popular options include:

ABC Radio: Australia's national broadcaster offers radio stations and podcasts in English.

SBS Radio: Offers multilingual broadcasts in several languages, catering to immigrants and non-English speakers.

Australian TV shows: Watching local programs like **Home and Away**, **Neighbours**, or news channels such as **ABC News** can help improve your listening comprehension of Australian English.

Transportation Booking Sites

1. Flights

Booking flights in advance is often the quickest and most efficient way to travel between Australia's major cities. Here are some of the best sites for booking domestic and international flights:

Webjet: One of Australia's leading travel booking platforms, Webjet allows you to compare flights from all major airlines, including budget options like Jetstar and Virgin Australia.

Website: www.webjet.com.au

Skyscanner: A popular international flight search engine, Skyscanner lets you compare prices from multiple airlines and travel agencies for both domestic and international flights.

Website: www.skyscanner.com.au

Qantas: Australia's flagship airline, Qantas offers flights to and from many international destinations, as well as across the country. Booking through their website ensures the best rates on their own flights.

Website: www.qantas.com

Virgin Australia: Another major airline in Australia, offering both domestic and international flights. Virgin Australia provides competitive prices, often with extra flexibility for bookings.

Website: www.virginaustralia.com

2. Trains

Traveling by train can be a scenic and comfortable way to explore Australia, especially if you are journeying between cities or to iconic destinations like the Great Ocean Road or the Outback.

V/Line: For travel within Victoria, V/Line offers train services to regional areas and beyond Melbourne. Tickets can be purchased online for specific routes or for flexible passes.

Website: www.vline.com.au

Great Southern Rail: For an iconic Australian train experience, Great Southern Rail offers long-distance services like The Ghan (Adelaide to Darwin) and the Indian Pacific (Sydney to Perth). These trains offer luxurious and scenic travel options.

Website: www.greatsouthernrail.com.au

NSW TrainLink: For travel across New South Wales, NSW TrainLink operates both regional trains and buses. Book tickets online or through their app for an easy journey.

Website: www.transportnsw.info

3. Buses

Australia has an extensive network of buses connecting major cities, regional towns, and remote locations. Bus travel can be a budget-friendly way to explore.

Greyhound Australia: Greyhound is one of the most recognized bus companies in Australia, offering intercity travel across the country. You can book individual tickets or passes for multiple journeys.

Website: www.greyhound.com.au

Murrays Coaches: Specializing in bus travel along the east coast, Murrays offers routes between Sydney, Canberra, Melbourne, and beyond, including transfers to major airports.

Website: www.murrays.com.au

Firefly Express: A budget bus service with routes linking Sydney, Melbourne, and Brisbane, Firefly Express is a great option for low-cost travel between major cities.

Website: www.fireflyexpress.com.au

4. Car Rentals

Renting a car offers flexibility for exploring Australia's vast landscapes, especially in more remote areas. Here are the best sites for booking rental cars:

Hertz Australia: A reliable international car rental service with locations across Australia. You can book everything from compact cars to luxury vehicles and campervans.

Website: www.hertz.com.au

Avis Australia: Another popular car rental company, Avis offers an extensive fleet and the ability to pick up and drop off cars at multiple locations across Australia.

Website: www.avis.com.au

Budget Australia: Ideal for budget-conscious travelers, Budget offers competitive rates and various vehicle types for self-drive holidays.

Website: www.budget.com.au

Europcar Australia: Known for quality and affordable car rentals, Europcar provides a wide range of vehicles for both short-term rentals and long-term trips.

Website: www.europcar.com.au

5. Ferries

Australia's coastline is beautiful and vast, and ferries are a great way to explore islands or coastal cities. Popular ferry routes include those to Tasmania and the Whitsundays.

Spirit of Tasmania: The most popular ferry service connecting mainland Australia (Melbourne) to Tasmania. It's the perfect option for travelers who want to take their car along for the ride.

Website: www.spiritoftasmania.com.au

Ferries to the Whitsundays: For access to the stunning Whitsunday Islands, book ferries through operators like Cruise Whitsundays, which run services between Airlie Beach and the islands.

Website: www.cruisewhitsundays.com.au

Sydney Ferries: For exploring Sydney Harbour and nearby coastal areas, Sydney Ferries provides a wide range of routes, from short trips to day excursions.

Website: www.transportnsw.info

6. Ride-Sharing and Taxis

For getting around cities or for short trips, ride-sharing and taxi services are widely available.

Uber: Available in most Australian cities, Uber is a convenient way to travel without the hassle of finding parking.

Website: www.uber.com

Ola: Another ride-sharing service, Ola operates in multiple cities across Australia and often offers competitive fares.

Website: www.olacabs.com

Taxicabs: Traditional taxis can be hailed on the street or booked via apps like 13CABS, which operates in most Australian cities.

Website: www.13cabs.com.au

Travel Blogs and Forums

1. Travel Blogs

Travel blogs are a great way to gather inspiration, detailed itineraries, and real traveler experiences. These bloggers often provide insider knowledge and recommendations for everything from must-see destinations to local eateries.

The Aussie Nomad: Focused on Australian travel, The Aussie Nomad offers a comprehensive guide to both iconic and off-the-beaten-path destinations. The blog also covers practical tips like driving distances and the best time to visit.

Website: www.theaussienomad.com

Australia's Guide: A blog dedicated to everything you need to know about traveling in Australia. It offers extensive information on accommodation, attractions, and adventure activities, alongside recommendations for local experiences.

Website: www.australiasguide.com

Nomadic Matt's Travel Blog: While not solely focused on Australia, Nomadic Matt offers a wealth of advice on traveling in Australia, including budget tips, itineraries, and suggestions for experiencing the country's natural beauty.

Website: www.nomadicmatt.com

The Culture Trip – Australia: The Culture Trip provides a diverse mix of travel advice, cultural experiences, and city guides. The Australian section is filled with travel ideas for art lovers, foodies, and nature enthusiasts.

Website: www.theculturetrip.com

The Blonde Abroad: This popular travel blog by a solo female traveler includes tons of tips for traveling through Australia, from luxury escapes to solo travel advice. It's especially useful for first-time visitors looking for a balance between adventure and relaxation.

Website: www.theblondeabroad.com

2. Travel Forums

Forums are ideal for gathering information from other travelers, asking questions, and getting personalized advice. They also offer up-to-date information on current conditions, events, and insider tips.

TripAdvisor Forums: The TripAdvisor community is vast, and their forums for Australia offer excellent advice for everything from city travel to unique experiences. Travelers post reviews, tips, and recommendations for destinations across the country.

Website: www.tripadvisor.com.au

Australia Travel Forum on Reddit: A lively subreddit for travelers discussing all aspects of traveling in Australia. Reddit's Australia Travel Forum is perfect for asking questions, finding local tips, and reading travel stories.

Website: www.reddit.com/r/AustraliaTravel

Lonely Planet's Thorn Tree Forum: Lonely Planet's renowned forum allows travelers to discuss their Australian travel experiences, seek advice, and exchange ideas. It's a great place to ask about local destinations, accommodations, and activities.

Website: www.lonelyplanet.com/thorntree

Australia.com Community Forum: Managed by Tourism Australia, this forum is a great resource for asking questions about Australian travel, finding tour operators, and reading blog posts from fellow travelers.

Website: www.australia.com

The Travel Hack Forum: A smaller but welcoming forum for travelers looking to discuss budget travel in Australia, unique off-the-beaten-path spots, and travel hacks.

Website: www.thetravelhack.com

3. Travel Communities

Facebook Groups: There are numerous Facebook groups dedicated to Australian travel, where travelers exchange advice, share photos, and help each other with planning. Some examples include "Backpacking Australia" and "Australia Travel Tips & Advice."

Search on Facebook: Australia Travel Groups

Tourism Australia's Official Website: For the most official and reliable travel information, Tourism Australia's website has guides and resources, including an interactive forum and useful links to blogs and forums.

Website: www.tourism.australia.com

Chapter 15: Conclusion
Final Tips for Traveling in Australia

1. Embrace the Vastness

Australia is the sixth-largest country in the world, and distances between key destinations can be huge. Plan your itinerary wisely, considering long travel times. Domestic flights are often the quickest way to cover vast distances, but for a more scenic experience, consider renting a car or taking a road trip.

2. Stay Sun Safe

Australia's sun can be intense, even during cooler months. Always wear sunscreen, sunglasses, and protective clothing when outdoors. Seek shade whenever possible, especially during peak sunlight hours from 10 AM to 4 PM.

3. Respect Local Wildlife

Australia is home to a variety of unique animals, but some can be dangerous if approached carelessly. Always follow local guidelines for interacting with wildlife, whether you're swimming with jellyfish in the Great Barrier Reef or encountering kangaroos in national parks.

4. Be Prepared for the Climate

Australia's climate varies greatly depending on the region. Northern areas like Queensland are tropical, while the southern parts, such as Tasmania, can be much cooler. Always pack according to the season and the specific region you'll be visiting.

5. Hydrate and Stay Energized

When traveling in remote or hot areas, especially in the outback, dehydration is a real risk. Always carry plenty of water, snacks, and sunscreen, particularly if you plan on hiking, road tripping, or exploring nature reserves.

6. Use Public Holidays to Your Advantage

Australia has several public holidays, such as Australia Day (January 26) and ANZAC Day (April 25). Many businesses may be closed on these days, so plan accordingly. Festivals and local events are often held during these times, which can offer unique cultural experiences.

7. Pack for Every Adventure

Australia offers a wide range of activities, from beach days and surf lessons to outback treks and city explorations. Be sure to pack versatile clothes that are suitable for both urban adventures and outdoor excursions. Don't forget comfortable walking shoes!

8. Learn About Indigenous Culture

Australia has a rich Indigenous heritage, and taking the time to learn about the Aboriginal and Torres Strait Islander cultures can enhance your travel experience. Many attractions, like the Uluru and Kakadu National Park, offer guided tours that provide insight into this ancient culture.

9. Respect the Environment

Australia is known for its stunning natural beauty. Practice eco-friendly travel habits by reducing waste, conserving water, and choosing sustainable accommodations and tours. Many areas, such as the Great Barrier Reef, rely on tourism to protect their ecosystems, so be a responsible traveler.

10. Enjoy the Aussie Spirit

Australians are known for their relaxed, friendly nature. Don't hesitate to strike up a conversation with locals—they're often happy to share their favorite spots, tips, and hidden gems. Whether you're in a bustling café or a remote outback town, embracing the laid-back Aussie spirit will make your trip even more memorable.

Embrace the Aussie Spirit

1. Be Open and Friendly

Australians are known for their easy-going nature, so don't be afraid to strike up a conversation with a local. Whether you're in a café, at a beach, or exploring a remote town, Aussies are often happy to share their tips, stories, and favorite spots. Embrace the casual, welcoming vibe by starting conversations and showing genuine interest in their culture and way of life.

2. Enjoy the Outdoors

Aussies love the outdoors, and the country's natural beauty is meant to be explored. Whether it's surfing on the Gold Coast, hiking through the Blue Mountains, or camping under the stars in the outback, Australians take full advantage of their breathtaking landscapes. Embrace the Aussie love for adventure and get outside to enjoy all that the country has to offer.

3. Celebrate with Locals

Australia is a land of festivals, sporting events, and celebrations. If you can, time your visit around events like the Sydney New Year's Eve fireworks, the Melbourne Cup, or the lively local festivals that take place across the country. These occasions are perfect opportunities to join in the Aussie spirit—whether you're dancing at a music festival, cheering for a sporting team, or enjoying a casual BBQ with friends.

4. Try Aussie Slang

While English is the official language, Aussies have a unique slang that adds a bit of fun and character to conversations. From "G'day mate" (hello) to "no worries" (it's all good), using a little Aussie lingo can make you feel more connected to the locals. Even if you don't master it, they'll appreciate the effort and likely help you learn along the way.

5. Be Laid-back

The Aussie spirit is all about taking things easy and not sweating the small stuff. While exploring, embrace the slower pace of life. Whether you're enjoying a quiet day at the beach, a leisurely walk through the bush, or an afternoon at a local pub, relax and soak in the natural rhythm of life in Australia.

6. Show Respect for Nature

Australians have a deep respect for their land, and this respect is ingrained in their culture. From the ancient wisdom of Indigenous Australians to the modern-day conservation efforts, nature holds a significant place in Aussie life. When visiting natural landmarks like Uluru or national parks, follow the guidelines, leave no trace, and appreciate the beauty that surrounds you.

7. Be a Responsible Traveler

Lastly, embracing the Aussie spirit means taking care of the environment and supporting sustainable tourism. Whether it's reducing waste, using eco-friendly products, or choosing sustainable travel options, showing respect for Australia's natural wonders will make you a part of the global effort to preserve its unique beauty.

Staying Safe and Enjoying the Journey

1. Be Sun-Smart

The Australian sun can be intense, especially in the summer months. Always wear sunscreen with high SPF, protective clothing, sunglasses, and a wide-brimmed hat. Try to avoid the sun between 10 AM and 4 PM when UV rays are at their strongest. Staying sun-smart will help prevent sunburns and heat-related illnesses.

2. Follow Local Guidelines for Wildlife Encounters

Australia is home to a wide range of unique wildlife, and while many animals are harmless, some can be dangerous if provoked. Always follow local instructions regarding wildlife—whether it's staying at a safe distance from kangaroos, avoiding swimming in jellyfish-prone waters (unless in designated areas), or respecting the habitats of crocodiles. Remember, some creatures are best admired from a distance.

3. Drink Plenty of Water

With Australia's often hot and dry climate, staying hydrated is key. Carry a water bottle and make sure you drink plenty of fluids, especially when exploring outdoor areas like the outback or national parks. Dehydration can sneak up on you, and being prepared with water can help you avoid feeling sluggish or unwell.

4. Keep Your Belongings Secure

Australia is generally safe, but like in any tourist destination, be mindful of your belongings. Use a money belt or a secure bag when out and about, especially in busy areas or tourist spots. Never leave valuables unattended on beaches or in cars.

5. Know Your Emergency Numbers

Australia's emergency services number is 000 (similar to 911 in the U.S.). Whether it's a medical emergency, fire, or police situation, dialing 000 will connect you with emergency services. It's also a good idea to familiarize yourself with the nearest hospital or medical center, especially if you're venturing into remote areas.

6. Stay Informed About Weather Conditions

Australia's climate can vary greatly depending on where you are, and weather conditions can change rapidly, especially in coastal and outback regions. Check weather forecasts before heading out, particularly if you're planning on hiking, camping, or engaging in water sports. Be aware of extreme weather events like bushfires, floods, or cyclones in certain seasons.

7. Know How to Get Around Safely

Australia is a vast country, and navigating its cities and rural areas requires some preparation. Always have a map or GPS system when driving, and make sure your rental car has a fully charged phone. If venturing into the outback or remote areas, carry extra fuel, food, and a satellite phone, as mobile service can be limited.

8. Choose Safe Outdoor Activities

While Australia offers incredible outdoor adventures, some activities come with inherent risks. If you're going scuba diving, surfing, or bushwalking, make sure you're with a reputable guide, especially if you're new to the activity. Adhere to safety instructions and use proper equipment to reduce the risk of accidents.

9. Respect Local Customs and Laws

Australia is a multicultural country with a strong respect for personal freedoms, but it's important to follow local customs and laws. Smoking is prohibited in many public areas, and littering carries fines. Respect Indigenous cultures, especially in sacred sites like Uluru, where climbing the rock is discouraged. Always ask permission before taking photos of people or cultural sites.

10. Trust Your Instincts

Above all, trust your instincts when it comes to safety. If something doesn't feel right, whether it's a location or a situation, take precautions and remove yourself from it. Australians are generally friendly and helpful, so don't hesitate to ask locals for advice or guidance if you're uncertain about anything.

Printed in Great Britain
by Amazon